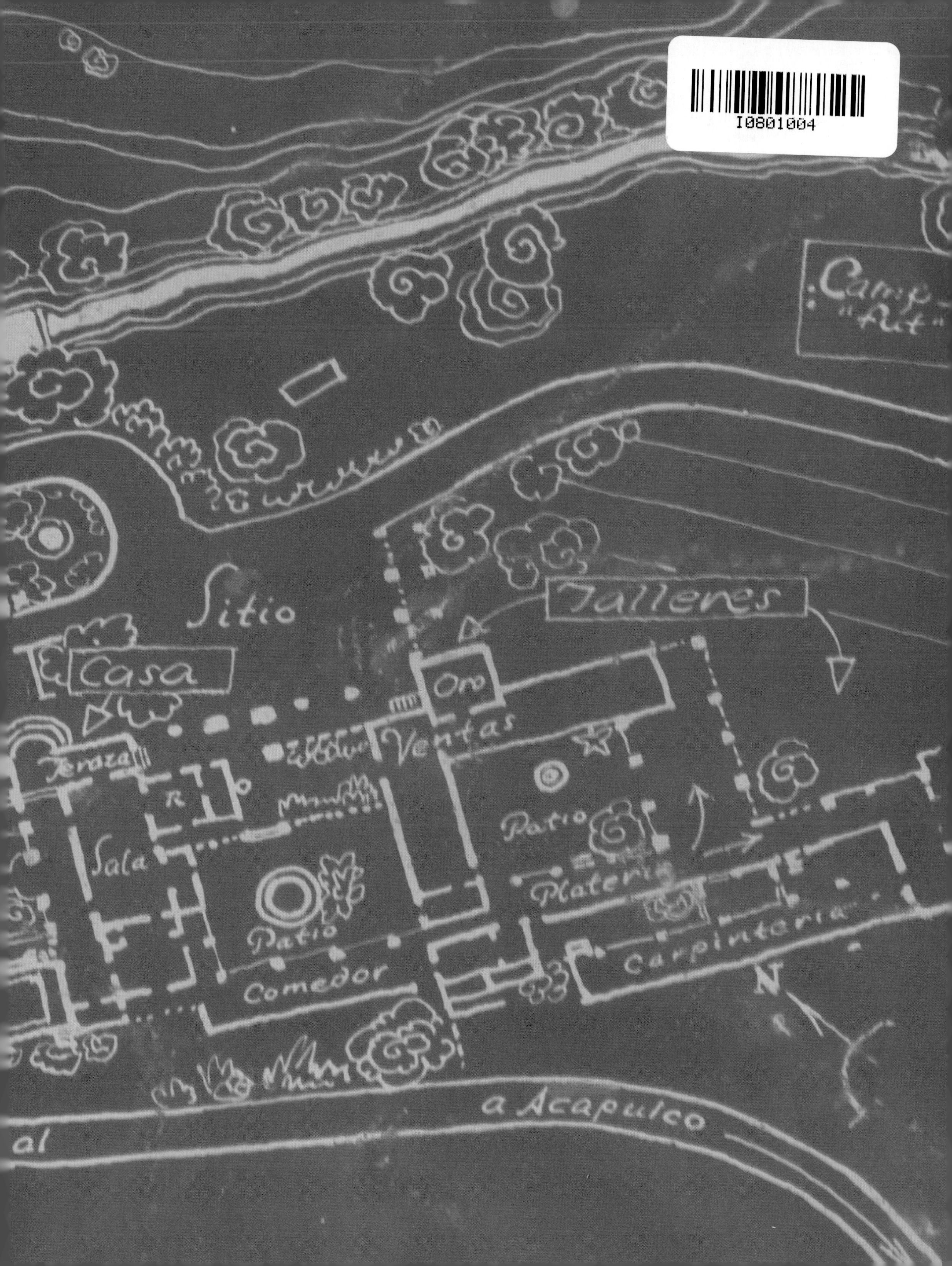
Camp-
"fut"
Sitio
Talleres
Casa
Oro
Ventas
Sala
Patio
Plateria
Patio
Comedor
carpinteria
N
a Acapulco
al

THE WILLIAM SPRATLING LEGACY

SANDY BAUM

THE WILLIAM SPRATLING LEGACY

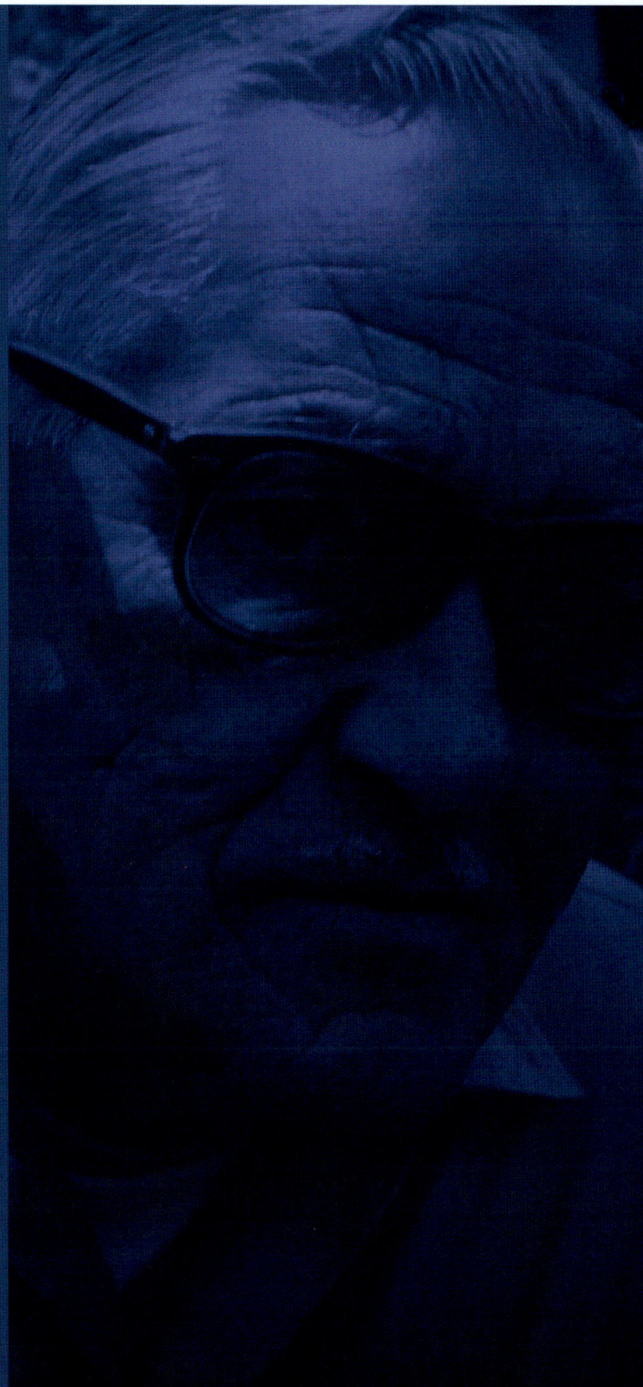

SANDY BAUM

Schiffer Publishing Ltd
4880 Lower Valley Road · Atglen, Pennsylvania 19310

Other Schiffer Books By The Author:
San Miguel's Mexican Interiors
San Miguel's Mexican Exteriors
Mexican Gardens & Patios
Colores: Mexican Interiors
Hammered Copper, Mexican Arts Series

Other Schiffer Books On Related Subjects:
Penny C. Morrill & Carole A. Berk. *Mexican Silver: Modern Handwrought Jewelry & Metalwork*
Penny C. Morrill. *Silver Masters of Mexico: Hector Aguilar & the Taller Borda*
Penny C. Morrill. *Margot Van Voorhies: The Art of Mexican Enameled Jewelry*
Leslie Piña. *Mexican Jewelry & Metal Art*
Leslie Piña. *Mexican Silver Jewelry Details*

Schiffer Books are available at special discounts for bulk purchases for sales promotions or premiums. Special editions, including personalized covers, corporate imprints, and excerpts can be created in large quantities for special needs. For more information contact the publisher:

Published by Schiffer Publishing Ltd.
4880 Lower Valley Road
Atglen, PA 19310
Phone: (610) 593-1777; Fax: (610) 593-2002
E-mail: Info@schifferbooks.com

For the largest selection of fine reference books on this and related subjects, please visit our web site at
www.schifferbooks.com
We are always looking for people to write books on new and related subjects. If you have an idea for a book, please contact us at the above address.

This book may be purchased from the publisher.
Include $5.00 for shipping.
Please try your bookstore first.
You may write for a free catalog.

In Europe, Schiffer books are distributed by
Bushwood Books
6 Marksbury Ave.
Kew Gardens
Surrey TW9 4JF England
Phone: 44 (0) 20 8392 8585; Fax: 44 (0) 20 8392 9876
E-mail: info@bushwoodbooks.co.uk
Web site: www.bushwoodbooks.co.uk

Library of Congress Control Number: 2011933376

Designed by RoS
Type set in VTCSwitchbladeRomance/NewBskvll BT

ISBN: 978-0-7643-3886-1
Printed in China

Contents

Foreword

William Spratling, architect and jewelry designer, is the father of the modern Mexican silver movement. His jewelry and home accessories boldly combined the clean lines of Art Deco and pre-Columbian motifs.

As two girls growing up in Taxco and at the former Spratling Ranch, we did not realize who or what was Spratling. As a matter of fact, we did not care for him or his designs; in a way we were angry at him for we had to clean all of the pieces of jewelry in the shop. But, otherwise, growing up at the ranch was quite an adventure; collectors, artists, and fabulous people were always around. To tell you the truth, as children we had no idea of what was going on, but it was a lot of fun.

William Spratling and our father, Alberto Ulrich, met in the 1950s. They were both collectors of pre-Columbian art and were also fascinated with Mexican history. Our father traveled all over Mexico and was an art dealer as well as a collector. As a result, we had art all over the place.

Our father became a very close friend of Spratling and they were always looking for new places to go and explore, such as the Real Balsas River and the Caves of Cacahuamilpa, looking for precious stones. They were also both passionate adventurers. They had some of the same interests and also found in Mexico a creative culture and a very concise workmanship in the local artisans. They both knew that this was a great beginning for a new generation in art history. We also think that they were a little crazy in their own way; Alberto owned and rode motorcycles and also raced Formula 3 automobiles, while Spratling had his own airplane and sailboat.

In 1945, Spratling flew to Alaska in his small plane on a fact-finding mission. He had been asked to write a program for the Alaska natives similar to the program he had created for his Mexican workers in Taxco. He was also asked to provide 200 models using Alaska's indigenous materials. Some of the indigenous materials he brought back in his plane. As part of the program he was asked to generate, a number of Eskimos were sent to the [Taxco] ranch to learn how to make those models under Spratling's tutelage and several maestros' supervision. In the end, the program that Spratling created for the Alaska natives was never funded and the models were sent back to the Smithsonian Institution where they now reside in a storage facility at the National Museum of the American Indian in Suitland, Maryland.

There is the funny story that our father once told us. Spratling, our father, and mother Carroll met for the first time at the Mexican comedian Cantinflas' house in Cuernavaca. Spratling was so stunned by our mother's beauty that he said that the only woman that would be allowed at the Spratling Ranch was Carroll.

Over the years as their friendship grew, my father kept asking Spratling to sell him the Ranch, and Spratling would always answer, "no." On August 7, 1967, Spratling was making a routine, early morning trip to Mexico City, when he crashed his car into a tree. He died in an ambulance on the way to the hospital. Taxco's residents as well as his long-time friends Diego Rivera, Siqueiros, Covarrubias and his former partner William Faulkner, were completely devastated with the news.

Elizabeth Anderson (Spratling's friend and the widow of Sherwood Anderson, the writer) wrote, "The town seemed to be in a state of shock. People stood around in little groups, not talking, just standing together, as if taking comfort in the mere presence of others. Large blue bows of ribbons were hung on all the doors of the shops and houses... the street sign for the Calle de Guillermo Spratling had been draped in black. In front of the church there were great banks of flowers. Enormous, heavy wheels of flowers, five feet tall had been propped up against the iron fence."

All the Tasquenians were draped in mourning. His workers took turns carrying his coffin to the colorful and picturesque cemetery. The day of Spratling's funeral was one of the saddest days in Taxco's history.

After Spratling's untimely death, our father purchased his estate to preserve his legacy. He acquired the ranch along with all of Spratling's molds and designs. Wanting to keep the quality and silver work up to Spratling standards, Alberto set up a new company, *Sucesores de William Spratling, S.A. de C.V.* and worked hard over the years to keep Spratling's legacy alive, until he, too, died in 2002.

We know that every design was taught very carefully by the hand of a genius. Every little thing in Mexico inspired Spratling: astrological symbols, mythological animals, architecture designs and pre-Columbian motifs were all inspirations for his work. He was also influenced by the surrealism in Europe, by the Mixtec and Zapotec treasures of Monte Alban in Oaxaca; by jaguars, dragonflies, and iguanas. Whatever his eyes captured he created in the most enthusiastic form.

Looking at these pieces of Spratling's designs all her life, Consuelo became more and more interested in making her own designs. She loves to mix all types of metals, stones, and leathers in the creation of a new design. She believes that all pieces are unique and that all people have an artist in them. Growing up with Spratling's collection and at times working in the silver shop gave her an inspiration to create her own line called "Stefano," named after our brother who died unexpectedly while on a trip to Hong Kong.

Time flew, and Violante left the ranch and went to study elsewhere in the world, ending up in San Antonio, Texas, where she graduated with an Arts degree. She then went to Paris where she worked in a gallery and took classes in restoration and design. A day Violante remembers, as if it were yesterday, was while doing a report on design for one of her art classes, and Spratling's designs came to mind. She then finally realized the beauty and elegance that he had in forming his pieces, and joy came to her heart. A few months later she moved from Paris back to Taxco and the ranch.

When Violante returned from Paris, she started working with our father in various aspects of the ranch and organized incredible shows of Spratling's work. Meanwhile, she started her own line of jewelry called, Violante's Designs. Her line became ever more popular because it was a real reminder that she had understood Spratling through design; everyone who saw her designs always said, "Oh your work reminds me so much of Spratling, but in a more contemporary way." She continues to create jewelry with her personal expression of everything that has influenced and inspired her.

Today, as a team, we are carrying on the Spratling legacy that our father sought to maintain after Spratling's death. We feel that Spratling was an amazing man who loved Mexico and its people. While he was alive, Spratling, or Don Guillermo as he was locally called, changed the economic and social life of Taxco and Mexican history forever.

We are working with one of Mexico's better known museums in Mexico City, The Franz Mayer Museum. It is known to have the best silver collection in Mexico, and today we have enriched their holdings with our father's collection of William Spratling's designs.

Violante & Consuelo Ulrich
Summer, 2011

Preface

I became interested in William Spratling's career when I moved to Mexico and began the study of Mexican folk art traditions first hand. I have made many new friends here, most of whom have been supportive in my endeavor to bring to the public photography-driven books about Mexico. As a result, working on this book has been a joy and a pleasure.

The first chapter gives an introduction to the town of Taxco, in the state of Guerrero, Mexico, where William Spratling came in 1929. Here he ignited a modern silver jewelry-making industry that has made Taxco famous today. William Spratling's original jewelry designs are discussed in the second chapter. They were made into silver objects in Taxco and sold at his shop, Las Delicias, and successfully in the United States in the early 1930s. A broad-brush look at the Spratling ranch is describe in the third chapter. William Spratling moved his design operations to the ranch after his company, Spratling y Artesanos, was taken away from him in 1945. Chapter 4 explores the two hundred designs William Spratling made between 1945 and 1949 for the U. S. Department of the Interior to stimulate craft production in Alaska. Chapter 5 looks at the jewelry-making company that Alberto Ulrich started in 1969, after Spratling's death, to continue the Spratling legacy. Prior to that time, Ulrich had acquired Spratling's house in Taxco. After Spratling's death, Ulrich also acquired Spratling's ranch outside Taxco where the silver workshop had been relocated since 1945. He had also acquired Spratling's designs, molds and hallmarks. The new company continued what Spratling had started, providing Spratling's designs to an interested and demanding public.

Today, the company Sucesores de Wm Spratling S.A. de C.V., is controlled and managed by Alberto Ulrich's two daughters. The legacy is firm and still evolving.

Acknowledgments

Books like this are not completed without assistance and contributions from many friends, relatives and interested persons one meets along the way. There are a few people I would like to thank for their involvement, no matter how insignificant they may think their contribution may be. Betsy January is probably my most vocal editor and critic. Barbara Guyton offered more than moral support when it was needed. My dear neighbor, Eugene Amador, offered an insight into the Mexican psyche. Violante Ulrich and Consuelo Ulrich, managing partners in Sucesores de William Spratling, S.A. de C.V., have provided many of the photographs and furnished information about Alberto Ulrich's past. Ken Van Wey is on the Indian Arts & Crafts board, U. S. Department of the Interior. Pat Nietfeld, PhD, is the Collections Manager at the Cultural Resource Center, National Museum of the American Indian, Suitland, Maryland. Nancy Newton has been helpful when she is in town between her worldly travels. A special thank you goes to my two editors at Schiffer Publishing, Ltd, Nancy Schiffer and Jeff Snyder, whose patience and foresight has brought this book into your hands.

INTRODUCTION

In 1926, William Spratling, was an associate professor of architecture at Tulane University in New Orleans. He traveled to Mexico to study its culture. In 1929, he moved to Taxco and was welcomed into the influential artistic circles of Mexico. U.S. Ambassador Dwight Morrow commented to Spratling at dinner one evening in 1930 that Taxco had been the site of silver mines for centuries, but unfortunately had never been considered a location where jewelry and objects of silver were designed and made. This seemingly insignificant comment changed the course of Taxco's artistic and economic history.

William Spratling was looking for a way to increase his income and discovered potential talent in the local workers. He motivated Taxco community artisans to create jewelry from his original designs and to rediscover the craft of silversmithing. He created an apprentice system for training young silversmiths with artistic talent and gave them the opportunity to develop their skills. He brought in from Iguala a highly regarded goldsmith to teach the art of working precious metal. The great beauty and craftsmanship that came from Taxco eventually earned the town worldwide recognition and fame for Mexico. Over the many subsequent years, some of these artisans opened workshops and stores of their own, a few being encouraged by Spratling's unwavering support.

Now considered to be great "old masters of Mexican silver," Hector Aguilar and Antonio Pineda along with former fellow apprentices of Spratling, including the Castillos, Ledesma, and Chino Ruiz, had produced some of the most highly regarded, collectable pieces of art, vases, serving sets and jewelry. Their work continues to inspire generations of silversmiths and artisans who now number in the hundreds.

William Spratling died on August 7, 1967, while driving his car just outside of Taxco. He swerved to miss a tree lying across the highway, but in so doing ran into a tree along the side of the roadway. The crash did not kill him, but on the way to the hospital in an ambulance he suffered a heart attack, from which he did not recover.

A silver bust of Spratling resides in Taxco's Silver Museum, alongside images of the famous Mexican, Don Jose de la Borda. William Spratling donated to the town of Taxco the pre-Columbian figures on display at the Museo Spratling behind the Santa Prisca Cathedral. However, according to Violante Ulrich, the silver designs in the same Spratling Museo house not Spratling originals, but copies of Spratling's silver designs made by a former craftsman at the ranch.

William Spratling almost single-handily transformed this sleepy mining town into a prosperous silver manufacturing center. The richness of Spratling's work and the quality of his designs has not diminished with time. Today, silver still drives the economy of Taxco. Many of the artisans who helped to make Taxco the popular destination it is today are no longer living, but their memories and major contributions to the local silver jewelry industry will not be forgotten.

CHAPTER 1

In 1716, Don Jose de la Borda, a Spaniard of French descent, discovered silver at Taxco, a small village along the Rio Balsas in the Tierra Caliente mountains. As legend has it, he was riding on horseback and, wandering in the hills around Taxco, spotted a rich silver vein. He made a fortune at Taxco and in gratitude built schools, roads, houses, and the beautiful and now-famous Santa Prisca Cathedral, ornate with gold leaf in the Spanish Baroque style. The church was begun around 1741 and consecrated in 1759. Don Jose's own son served as a priest there. The church can be seen from anywhere in Taxco. It glitters in the sunlight and has become a focal point for the town. Don Jose is still considered the "father" of the town.

In modern time, Mexico underwent a social revolution that began in 1910 and resulted in a new government and Constitution in 1917. The average Mexican villagers were impoverished at the time and reforms took another generation to develop. Inspired leaders gradually exposed triumphs in Mexican history to empower the population and reconstruct a future.

In 1921, a Summer School for Foreigners was started by the Mexican National University, offering courses in Mexican history, archaeology and folklore. North American intellectuals came to Mexico to be part of the social changes they thought to be taking place there. They hoped to gain an understanding of the culture and plan for future cooperation between the United States and Mexico. Some sought commercial gains and some historical perspective.

Into this stimulating atmosphere William Spratling found opportunity and historical passion that defined the rest of his life and left an indelible influence on the town of Taxco.

Today, Taxco sits on a hill in the Mexican state of Guerrero, southwest of Mexico City. It is one of the oldest mining towns in Mexico and has retained its natural charm with colonial ambiance, white painted houses, red tile roofs, cobble-stone, narrow winding streets and the old, towering Santa Prisca Cathedral.

TAXCO

LEGACY

William Spratling. Courtesy of Sucesores de Wm Spratling, S.A. de C.V.

Taxco.

The Guadalupe Chapel, built in 1877.

A street in Taxco with a view approaching Santa Prisca.

Rounding a curve, the first view of Taxco.

Typical street views in Taxco.

HOTEL MELENDEZ
RESTAURANT
PAELLA

Taxco city center and the Santa Prisca Cathedral.

Interior view of Santa Prisca. There are a number of altar pieces that reach from floor to ceiling, all covered in gold leaf.

Santa Prisca Cathedral's façade.

The zocalo, or main plaza, in front of the Santa Prisca Cathedral, sometimes referred to as Borda Plaza after the Frenchman who built the church.

CHAPTER 2

Respected epileptologist William P. Spratling, who had been raised outside Auburn, Alabama, was living with his wife, son David, and daughters Lucille and Wilhelmina, in Sonyea, Livingston County, New York, when his son, William, was born on September 22, 1900. Young William did not have a sweet childhood. He attended Calvert grammar school in Baltimore, Maryland, in 1910, and was in Summit, New Jersey, in 1911 and '12 when his mother and sister, Wilhelmina, both died. He went to live with an uncle until 1914, when his father died. Then he lived near his father's home area near Auburn, Alabama, and attended Auburn High School, from which he graduated in 1918.

William Spratling excelled in his studies and entered Auburn Polytechnic School to study architecture. He used his free time well and became a summer draftsman in Birmingham, Alabama, while he was in college. He became an instructor at Auburn Polytechnic from 1919 to 1921.

Next, he used his training and love of history at Tulane University in New Orleans, Louisiana, as an Associate Professor in Architecture from 1922 until 1929. During that time he wrote articles on architecture, a book on pencil drawing, and illustrated the book *Picturesque New Orleans*. He was becoming part of the art community in New Orleans and an intellectual. He traveled to France in the summer of 1923 and to Italy in 1924. From 1926 to 1929, William Spratling attended lectures on architecture given in Mexico City at the National University of Mexico. He loved the history, architecture, and folk arts and spent more time outside Mexico City. His article "Some Impressions of Mexico" appeared in *Architectural Forum* in 1927, and other writing about old architecture was becoming a steady interest.

American Frederick W. Davis, "discovered and fostered native [Mexican] folk art and the work of Mexican contemporary artists and participated in the development of a crafts industry which would include the production of silver jewelry." (Morrill and Berk, *Mexican Silver*, p. 24) Davis ran the Sonora News Company gift shop in the Palacio Iturbide Hotel in Mexico City and featured art works and Mexican crafts. In 1927, he and his employee, René d'Harnoncourt, compiled the first exhibition of contemporary painters. Davis stimulated Mexican craft production, including feather painting and lacquer work, with local artists, especially from 1927 to 1933. Fred Davis sold Americans Elizabeth and Dwight Morrow, the American Ambassador to Mexico, a house, Casa Mañana, in Cuernavaca, and helped to decorate it and form a collection of folk and colonial art for him. In 1928, William Spratling helped Fred Davis with renovations to the house. Spratling's exposure to Mexican arts sealed his artistic passion.

William Spratling came to Taxco in 1929 to make a living. The area was impoverished and isolated in the mountains. He bought a little house on the Calle de Las Delicias as a start. His knowledge of silver in the region intrigued him, and he wanted to stimulate crafts among the local people. Gradually, to recreate a long-abandoned silver industry there, he found in Iguala a young silversmith, Artemio

William Spratling with his workshop team. Courtesy of Sucesores de Wm Spratling, S.A. de C.V.

IGINAL DESIGNS

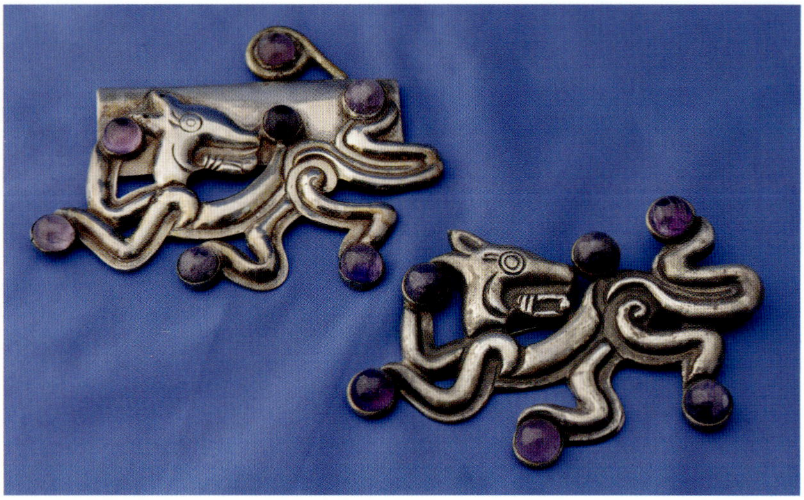

William Spratling. Silver coyotes with amethyst, One is a purse clip and the other a brooch, c. 1944.

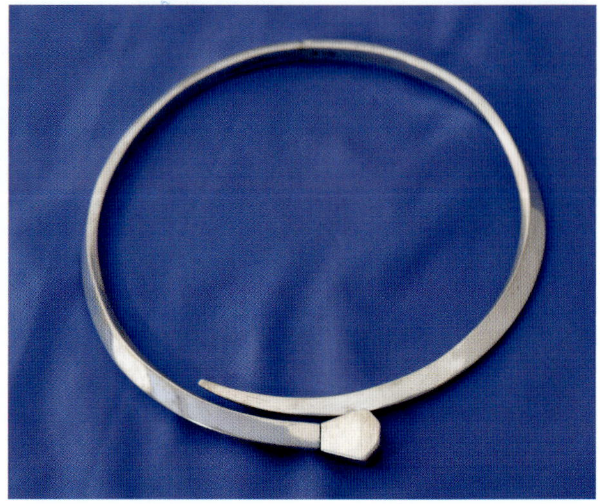

William Spratling. Choaker necklace, silver.

Navarrete, who he brought to Taxco in 1930 to teach silversmithing to local men. As they learned the trade, they sold their results in a little shop called "Las Delicias."

William Spratling's original designs for the silver objects derived from ancient and traditional Mexican roots and his sense of proportion, balance and form. Many of the pieces were made in the likeness of mythical or semi-mythical animals. The butterfly, a popular motif in Mexican art, has had special meaning since the time of the Aztecs. They believed the butterfly represented the souls of women who had died in child birth or warriors who had died on the battlefield.

As the silver objects and jewelry were gradually constructed, his workshop became known as the Taller de Las Delicias, from 1931 to 1945. Later they were made at his ranch at Taxco-el-Viejo, from 1945 to 1967.

Many artisans worked for William Spratling through the years from 1931 to 1967. Among the silver workers he trained and hired were young boys who learned their trades and stayed at his workshops for many years, as well as those who later started their own workshops in Taxco. Of the latter group, Hector Aguilar was Spratling's workshop manager in 1939. Antonio Castillo, Valentín Vidurreta, Antonio Pineda, and Sigi Pineda, as well as many others, learned silversmithing at Taller de Las Delicias. Many of the silver workers became masters of Mexican designs as their work progressed during the 1940s.

When retail stores in New York City and elsewhere could not procure fine silver and jewelry from Europe in the early 1940s, buyers looked to Mexico and William Spratling to fill their shelves. The market was ripe for consumer goods of their type, and Spratling had the connections to the art world in the United States to satisfy the demand. His business grew as his silversmiths improved their skills.

In 1944, William Spratling sold shares in a new company he formed with his employees, Spratling y Artesanos. He provided a means for the workers to share in both the success of their work and the responsibility of running the company.

The Spratling designs represent some of over five hundred items he created over his thirty-seven years at Taxco. Spratling's designs were of a clean architectural quality, employing pre-Columbian and original motifs. He used either plain silver or silver combined with wood, tortoise shell or semi-precious stones found in the local area. Spratling's designs from the 1930s through the1960s have become collector's items, with many now found in U.S. museums and important private collections.

William Spratling. Provincial set consisting of coffee pot, creamer and sugar bowl, in silver and wood.

William Spratling. Cream pitcher, silver with a wooden handle.

William Spratling. Candle holders, silver

William Spratling. Silver dish

William Spratling. Silver pitcher.

William Spratling. Ash tray of silver, on three carved Jaguar-shaped legs and a wooden base.

William Spratling. Detail of the jaguar legs.

William Spratling. Owl pin with amethyst eyes, silver, c. 1943.

William Spratling. Salt bowl, silver, with wooden spoon.

William Spratling. Six-pointed star pin with amethyst inlaid at three points and the center, silver.

William Spratling. Pin of Mexican design, silver.

William Spratling. Pin in the shape of a monkey, pre-Columbian design, silver c. 1930.

William Spratling. Quetzalcoatl pin of Mexican design, c. 1942,

William Spratling. Letter opener, wood and silver.

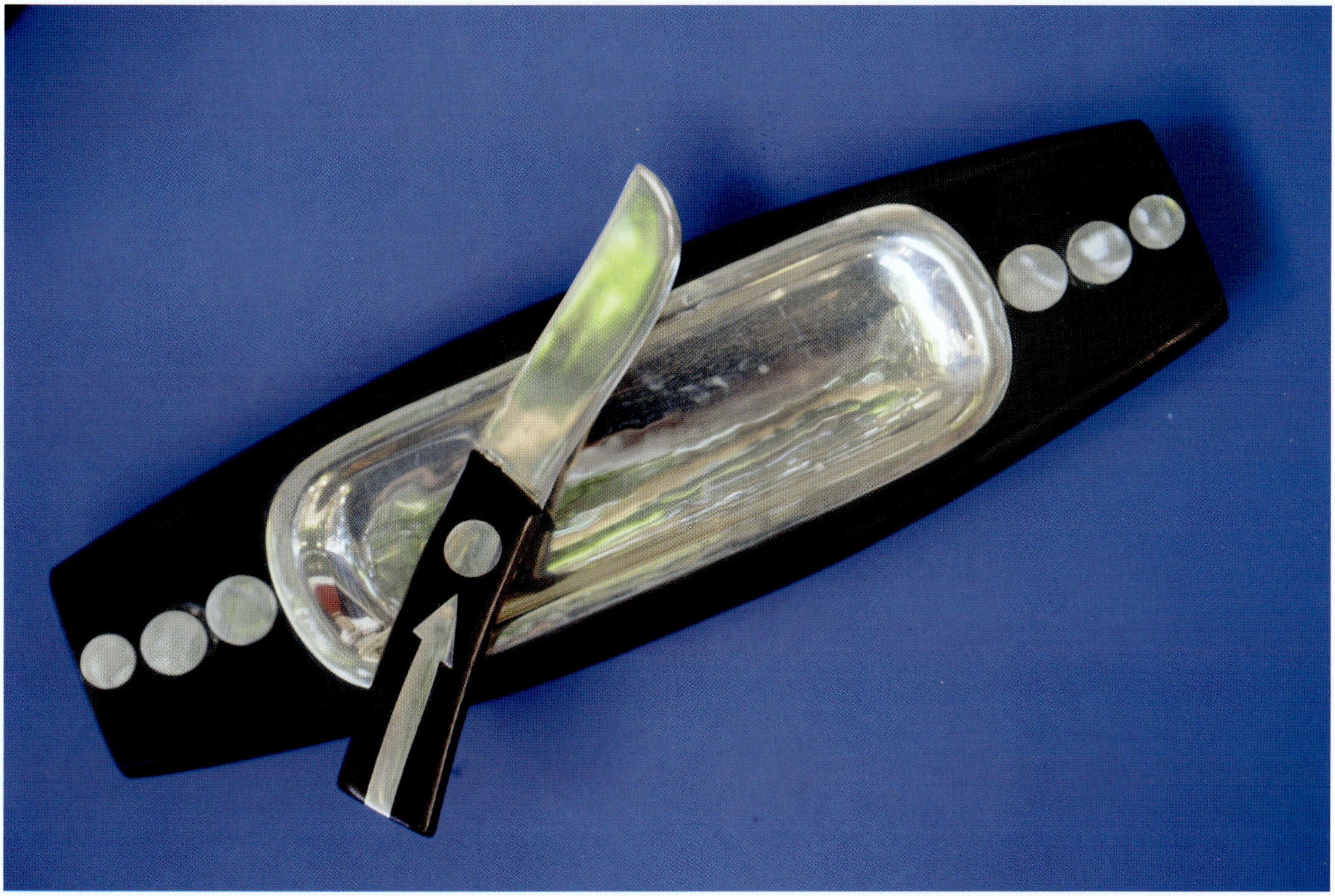

William Spratling. Ebony and silver butter dish and butter knife, c. 1958.

William Spratling. Bracelets, pre-Columbian designs, silver, c. 1935-45.

William Spratling. X-O bracelet, pre-Columbian design, silver, c. 1935-45.

William Spratling. Earrings of silver.

William Spratling. Cuff bracelet with amethyst inlaid circles, silver, c. 1940.

William Spratling. Cuff bracelet with ebony and silver.

William Spratling. Cigarette box, rectangular with hinged top, 18K gold dots, and silver.

William Spratling. Cigarette box, hexagonal with hinged top, silver.

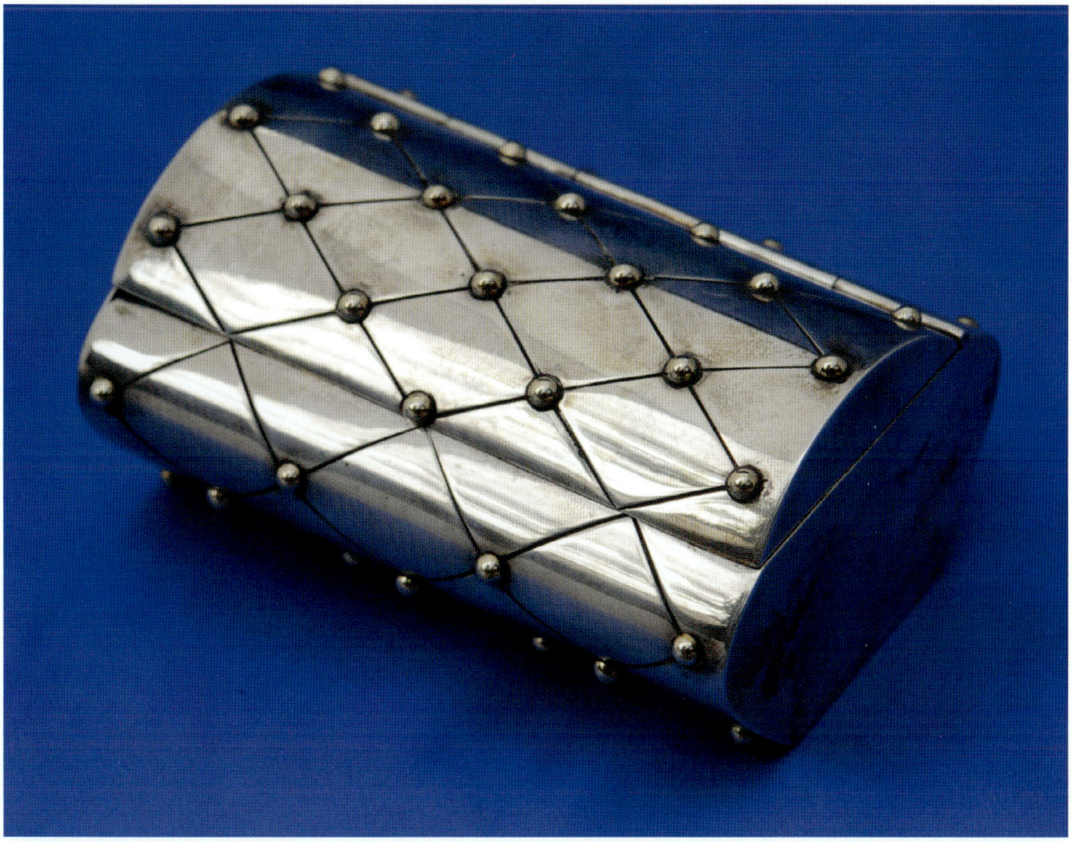

William Spratling. Cigarette box, rectangular with hinged barrel top, silver.

William Spratling. Cigarette box, rectangular with diamond design, hinged top, silver, c. 1930.

William Spratling. Necklace of light, thin silver, c. 1940.

William Spratling.
Cross pendant, silver.

William Spratling. Bracelet, silver, c. 1935-1945.

William Spratling. Cuff bracelet, silver.

William Spratling. Cuff bracelet, silver and copper.

William Spratling. Bracelet of pre-Columbian design, silver, c. 1945-1950.

William Spratling. Pill box in the shape of a fish, flexible body and hinged head, silver, c. 1950.

William Spratling. Earrings, pre-Columbian design, silver, c. 1930.

William Spratling. Earrings, seven circles design, silver.

William Spratling. Bar pin in the shape of two peacocks, silver, c. 1935.

William Spratling. Earrings, two circles banded together, silver.

William Spratling. Link bracelet, silver.

William Spratling. Belt buckle, silver.

William Spratling. Link bracelet, silver.

William Spratling. Finger ring, pre-Columbian design, jade and 18K gold.

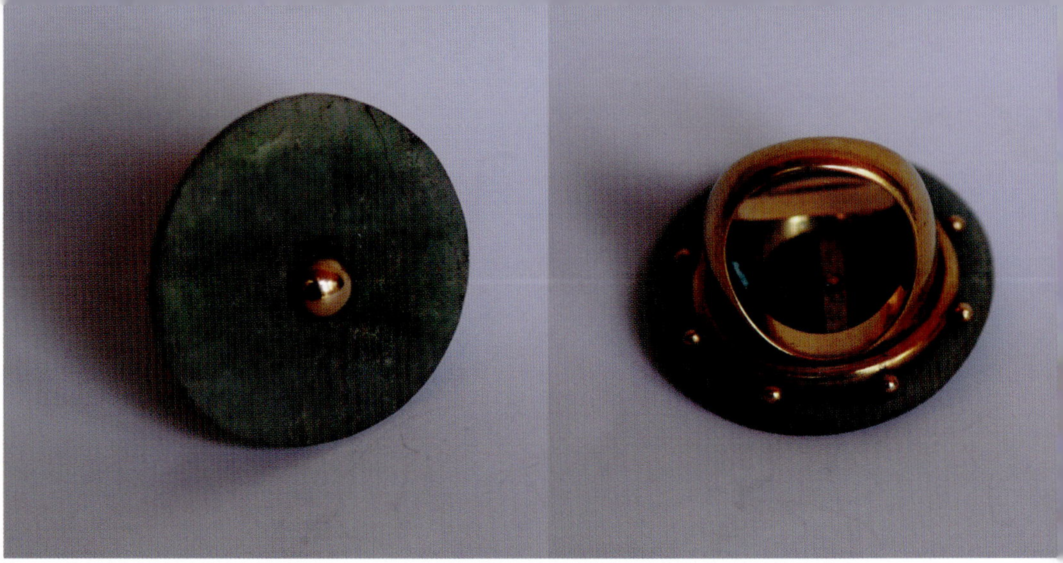

William Spratling. Finger ring, pre-Columbian design and jade, 18K gold, front and back views.

William Spratling. Cuff bracelet, silver.

William Spratling. Cuff bracelet and earrings, tortoise shell and silver, c. 1930.

William Spratling. Brooch of pre-Columbian design with carved jaguar face, jade and 18K gold, c. 1930-1940.

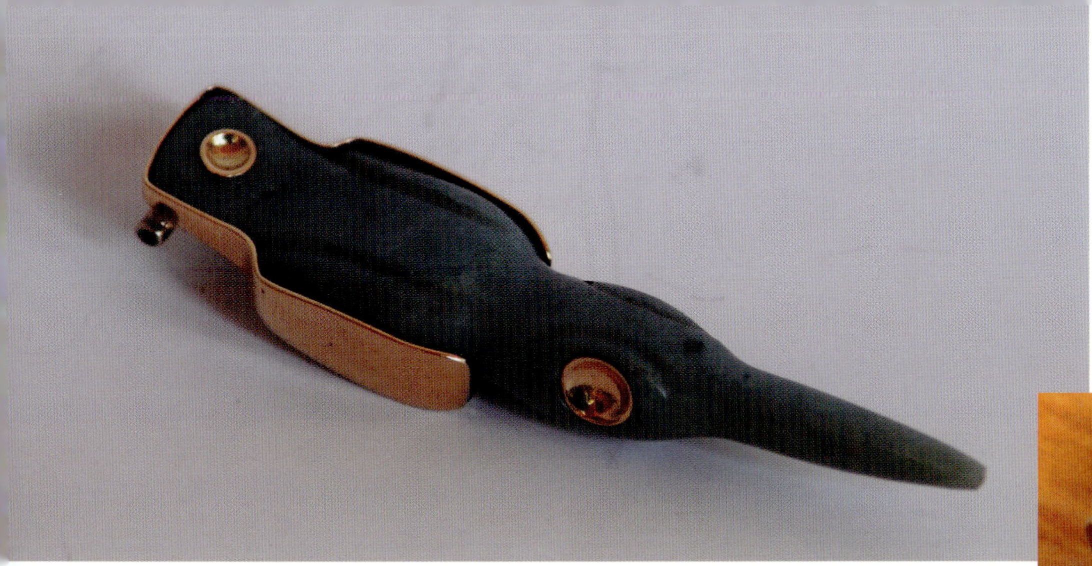

William Spratling. Pendant in the shape of a hummingbird, pre-Columbian design, jade and gold, c. 1930-1940.

William Spratling. Cuff bracelet, silver, c. 1940.

William Spratling. 5-piece place setting of silver flatware inlaid with 18K gold.

William Spratling. Pin, pre-Columbian design, silver and copper, c. 1935.

William Spratling. Original design drawing with a pre-Columbian motif.

William Spratling. Brooch in the shape of a star with malachite and silver, c 1940.

William Spratling. Pin, pre-Columbian design, silver, c. 1935.

William Spratling. Two pins in the shape of dragonflies with tortoise shell wings, silver, c. 1950.

William Spratling. Earrings with ebony discs and silver, c. 1935-40.

William Spratling. Earrings with pre-Columbian bird design, blue jade and silver, c. 1940.

William Spratling. Necklace of pre-Columbian style with jade and bone beads and 18K gold.

William Spratling. Necklace of jade and glass beads with 18K gold and an Olmec engraved stone.

William Spratling. Belt buckle, silver, c. 1950.

William Spratling. Necklace of ceramic, gold, coral and turquoise beads.

William Spratling. Cuff bracelet, with amethyst inset dots, silver, c. 1940.

William Spratling. Original drawing showing a candle holder with ebony base. Courtesy of Sucesores de William Spratling, S.A. de C.V.

William Spratling. Necklace with blue malachite, silver, c. 1950.

William Spratling. Necklace with amethyst in three drops as small bells, silver, c. 1945-1950.

William Spratling. Necklace of two strands
with small balls of amethyst and silver, c. 1943.

William Spratling. Necklace in bow design with tortoise shell and silver, c. 1940.

William Spratling. Necklace with ebony and silver, c. 1935-1940.

William Spratling. Original design drawing.
Courtesy of Sucesores de Wm Spratling, S.A. de C.V.

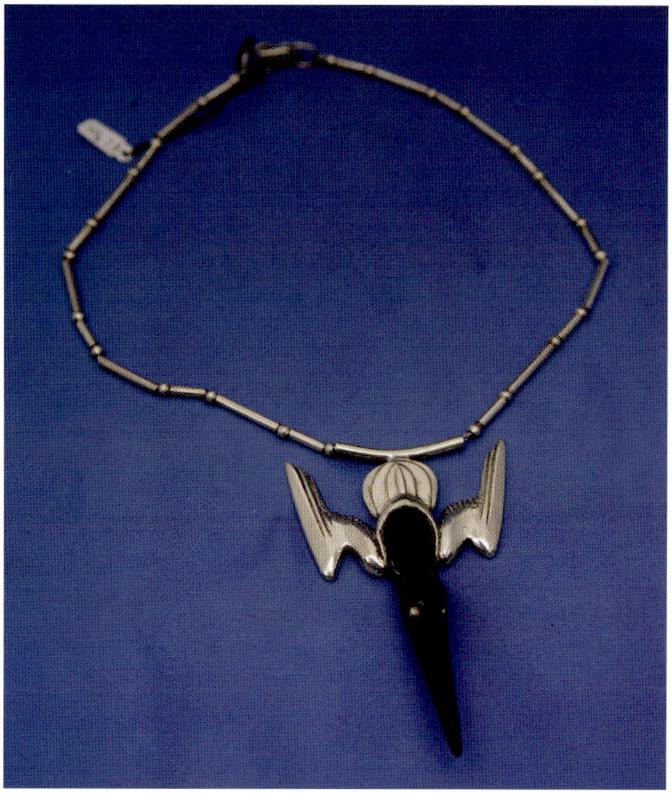

William Spratling. Necklace with hummingbird pendant, obsidian and silver, c. 1955.

William Spratling. Necklace with hummingbird pendant variation, silver, c. 1955.

William Spratling. Necklace with pretzel design, tortoise shell and silver, c. 1935-1940.

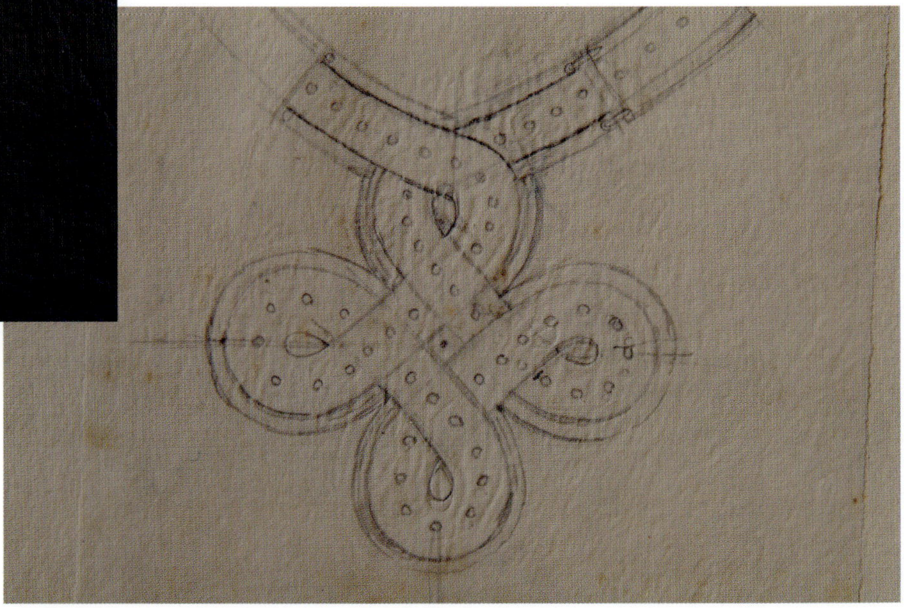

William Spratling. Original pretzel design drawing. Courtesy of Sucesores de Wm Spratling, S.A. de C.V.

Detail, necklace with pretzel design, tortoise shell and silver.

Detail, necklace, silver, c. 1940.

William Spratling. Necklace, silver, c. 1940.

Detail, necklace with tortoise shell and silver, c. 1940.

William Spratling. Necklace with tortoise shell and silver, c. 1945-1950.

William Spratling. Necklace, pre-Columbian design, silver, c. 1945-1950.

William Spratling. Bracelet matching the necklace.

William Spratling. Necklace, silver, c. 1942-1950.

William Spratling. Necklace with half-moon center, silver, c. 1950.

William Spratling. Original design for a spoon resembling Alaskan styles, 1940s. Courtesy of Sucesores de Wm Spratling, S.A. de C.V.

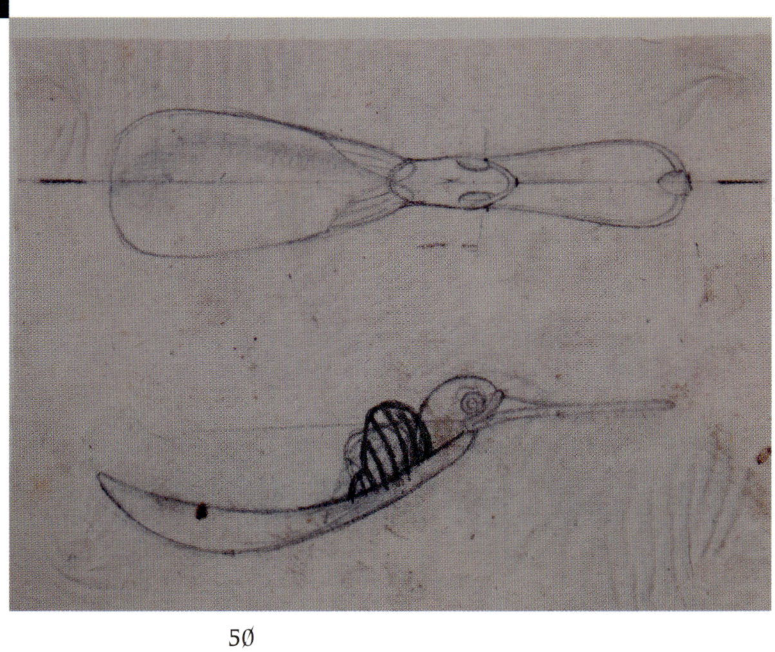

William Spratling. Alaskan Mask necklace, not one of the Alaskan models, but inspired by masks he saw in Alaska, with ivory, tortoise shell and silver, c. 1949.

William Spratling. Original design drawing. Courtesy of Sucesores de Wm Spratling, S.A. de C.V.

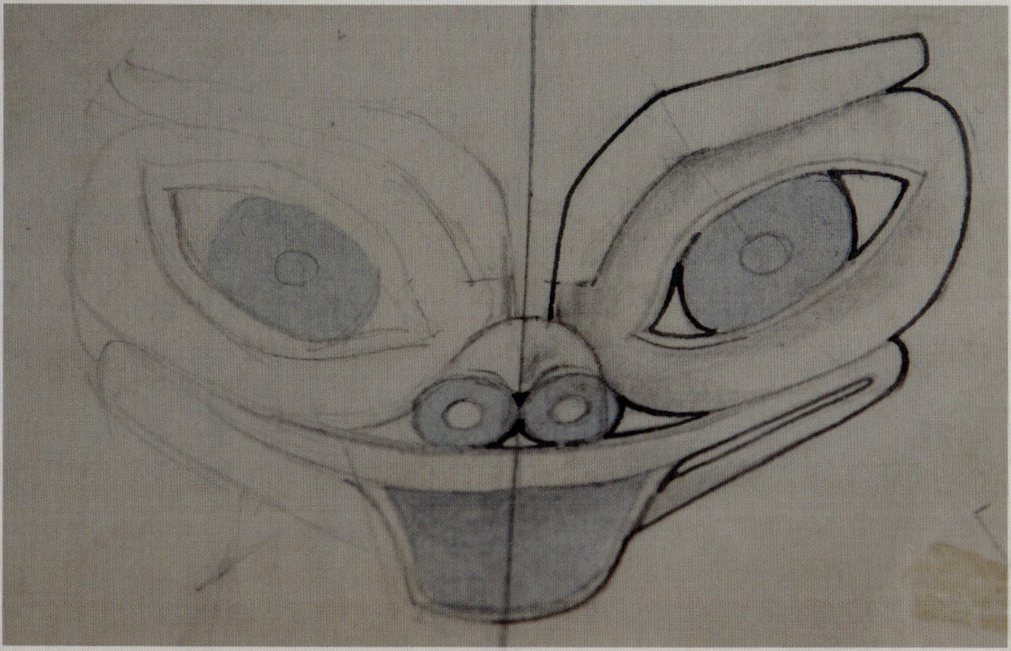

CHAPTER 3

THE RANCH

In 1945, William Spratling moved the silver working operations to this ranch, after resigning as Director of Spratling y Artesanos.

The ranch is located at Taxco-el-Viejo, about a twenty-minute drive south of Taxco, at an 1800 feet lower elevation. The driveway and garden paths are still lined with some of William Spratling's pre-Columbian stone figure collection. The compound is unpretentious, rustic, Mexican-ranch style that fits the surroundings.

Here Spratling carried on his workshop and trained new workers for their jobs for over twenty years. During this period in his career, William Spratling was engaged in a project to stimulate similar crafts for the native people of Alaska (see Chapter 4). He continued to study, locate and collect pre-Columbian sculpture and art works, and from them devised his own new designs for silver goods. He shared many adventures with his friend, Alberto Ulrich, who likewise was passionate about history and Mexican folk arts.

The old swimming pool that Spratling had built at the ranch lays dormant today, but still contains water. The many trees that Spratling had planted have taken over the area surrounding the pool, and therefore make it too shady for swimming. Alberto Ulrich had another pool built after he assumed ownership in 1969, within the compound at a place devoid of trees and shade.

In August of 2009, the old workshop, the focus of former energy and concentration, was still being used to make jewelry by the hands of Dom Tomas Vega, while modern machinery sat idle. A huge safe, off in a side room, sat open exposing some relics of Spratling's former collections. The old dining table was still in place, as a reminder of the many fascinating people and events that had occurred around it.

William Spratling and Carroll Ulrich at the Spratling ranch. Courtesy of Sucesores de Wm Spratling, S.A. de C.V.

Alberto Ulrich with silversmith Dom Tomas Vegas.

Detail of a light fixture in the opening above the main entrance.

Detail of one of the pedestrian entries.

Original vehicle entrance designed by Alberto Ulrich in 1981, sometime after he moved to Taxco-el-Viejo.

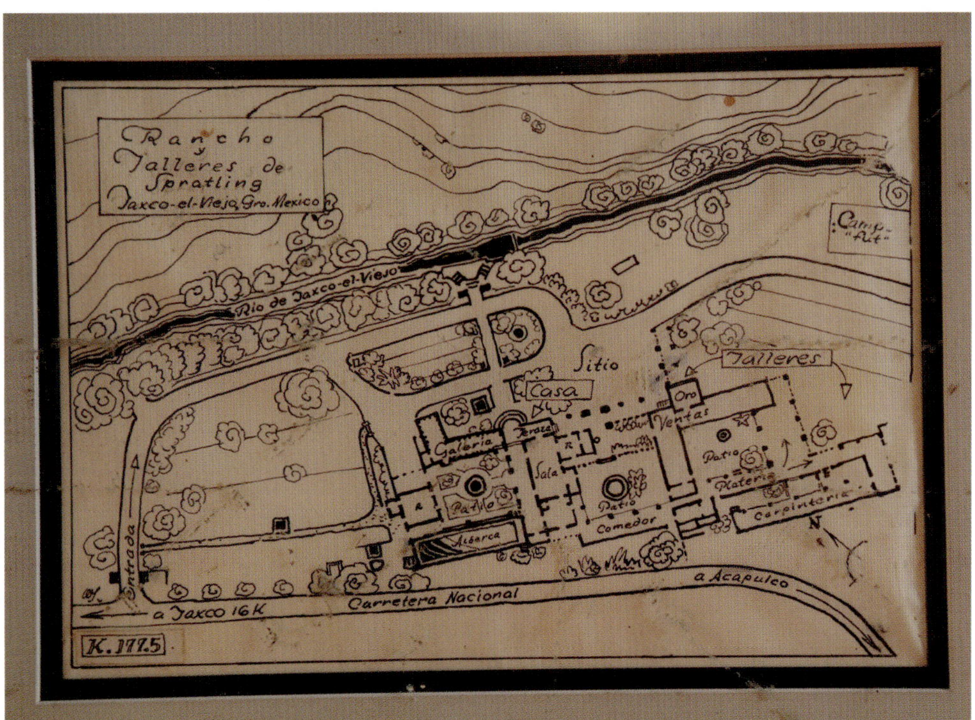

Map of the Spratling ranch at Taxco-el-Viejo.

Inside the ranch as one approaches the main gate that Alberto Ulrich designed.

A treehouse that Alberto Ulrich built for his children. This escape-to building hangs out over the river that flows along the east side of the ranch property.

Silversmith Don Tomas Vega's residence near the entrance to the ranch.

The primary pedestrian entrance that was designed by William Spratling in 1950.

Alberto Ulrich's second-floor office.

Guesthouse bedroom.

Stairs to the upper deck and original pool area.

A typical exterior view.

Stairs to the second floor bedrooms.

Arched loggia outside William Spratling's former, on-site museum.

Interior view of William Spratling's former, on-site museum.

Upper deck outside Alberto Ulrich's office.

View through the trees to one of the many upper decks.

Stairs to the upper deck.

Wooden corner cabinet designed and built by William Spratling.

Typical patterned saltillo tile floor installed by Alberto Ulrich.

A motor-driven stamping machine in the ranch workshop.

This machine was used to reduce the size of wires by pulling or drawing them through ever-decreasing sized holes until the desired size was achieved.

In the foreground, a manual press for pushing flat sheet silver into molds.

William Spratling. Cuff bracelet in silver, c. 1940, resting on the old workbench.

A capuccino cup holder, part of a set designed for the Marquessa Hotel.

William Spratling. Two necklaces of wood and gold, that were found in the vault at the ranch.

An ancient, carved stone of the Olmec civilization.

A carved stone fragment.

An old statue of carved stone.

A sphere of solid stone.

A cross carved in old stone; it may have been a grave marker.

A pot with a lid, from Michoacan. This piece is from Alberto Ulrich's former shop, Milagros, in San Antonio, Texas.

Old Aztec figure carved in cantera.

A clay pot from Alberto Ulrich's former folk art shop, Milagros, in San Antonio, Texas.

An old ceramic base in the shape of a fish, from Alberto Ulrich's shop, Milagros, in San Antonio.

A water jug from Alberto Ulrich's pre-Columbian collection.

A lobster design on a ceramic vessel from Alberto Ulrich's pre-Columbian collection.

William Spratling rescued this bronze bell when he moved from Taxco to the ranch. The bell had been cast in 1944 for the opening of his shop at La Florida, and has inscriptions commemorating the founding of Spratling y Artesanos, with the year 1944 as well as his hallmark, WS.

A figure carved in old volcanic rock.

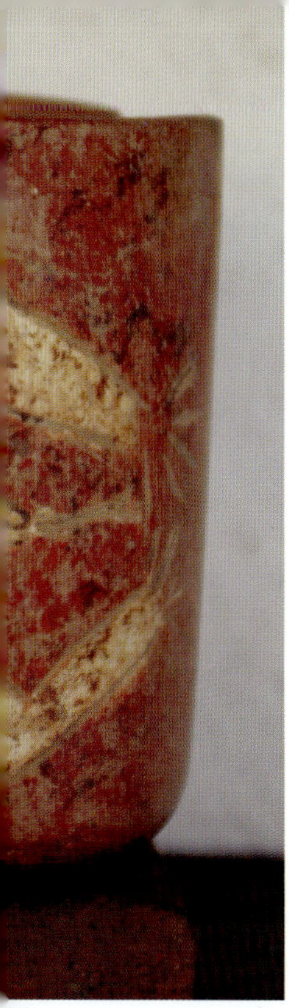

A long-necked vessel from Alberto Ulrich's pre-Columbian collection.

A short-necked vessel from Alberto Ulrich's pre-Columbian collection.

An old stone figure.

A figure of cantera stone, formerly part of William Spratling's original art collection.

A seated figure in clay, from Alberto Ulrich's pre-Columbian collection.

Masks of clay from Alberto Ulrich's collection.

William Spratling's stylized hallmark design sitting on a grate. The design was adapted in silver by Alberto Ulrich at some time in the 1990s.

CHAPTER 4

After his success in organizing the indigenous group of workers in Mexico, William Spratling was asked to create designs for an Alaskan native program.

In 1945, he was approached by two friends from his earlier days, René d'Harnoncourt, Director of the Department of the Interior's Arts & Crafts Board (IACB) and Ernest Gruening, Governor of the territory of Alaska. They wanted Spratling to create a plan for training Alaska's natives and Eskimos to design and fabricate silver jewelry and objects based on their traditional designs using indigenous materials.

Ernest Gruening had been a journalist who went to Mexico for six months in 1922 to write a series of articles for the magazine *Colliers*. He wrote the book *Mexico and Its Heritage,* published in 1928, where, according to Helen Delpar, he is quoted: "...one cannot escape in Mexico's everyday life the all-pervading manifestations of the persistent native culture." [Morrill, *Mexican Silver*, p.16]

Spratling's 1945 report, which he wrote as his plan for organizing the crafts in Alaska and that he submitted to the U. S. Department of the Interior, is presented in its entirety in the Appendix.

As part of the contract he was offered, and that Spratling eventually signed, he produced in 1949 two hundred models of his designs for the future Alaskan craftsmen to use. When he completed the models, they were shipped to Washington, D.C. and put on display. Then they were sent to New York for a show and finally to Alaska for another show. After the show in Alaska, the models were returned to the Department of the Interior's Indian Arts & Crafts Board where they languished for 51 years. By an act of Congress, the models were transferred to the Smithsonian Institution's National Museum of the American Indian Cultural Resource Center in Suitland, Maryland, on January 1, 2000.

The Cultural Resource Center has an inventory of the items received from the IACB that shows eighty-eight inventory numbers, with some of the inventory numbers embracing four, five or six items, such as a set of five buttons, or a service set of four, five or six eating utensils. Each piece constituted one of the original two hundred models. While a set of five buttons was listed as one inventory number, those items made up five of the original 200 models, not one.

In her book, *William Spratling and the Mexican Silver Renaissance* (page 21), guest curator Penny Morrill wrote, "In 1994, after much searching to discover the location of Spratling's Alaska pieces, I published the list of designs in the hope that it might spark recognition. Seven years later, two of the pieces were brought into the Alaska State Museum for evaluation. I was able to identify them; they were purchased by the museum."

THE ALASKA C

William Spratling, in the center, with acquaintances, 1940s. Courtesy of Sucesores de Wm Spratling, S.A. de C.V.

ONNECTION

The Alaskan Models List

The original list that William Spratling sent to William Warne, Assistant Secretary at the U. S. Department of the Interior, is dated April 18, 1949. The list was titled "The Alaskan Models" by authors Penny Morrill and Carole Berk, in their book *Mexican Silver* (1994-2007, pp 260-261).

The National Museum of the American Indian (NMAI) Cultural Resource Center, in Suitland, Maryland, provided an inventory that lists the pieces it received from the United States Department of the Interior's Indian Arts and Crafts Board on January 1, 2000. Items missing from the NMAI inventory, and the two original items now in the Alaska State Museum, are included on this list from William Spratling. The missing Alaska models were identified by comparing the NMAI photo list with the Spratling list. The number of models missing from the original 200 is based on this comparison; it totals 32.

The original list of models from Spratling actually totals 212 items, if you assume each entry of cuff links or earrings includes two pieces. But Spratling does not use the term "pair," as he does when referring to a button "set," or he uses multiple numbers indicating more than one item in that listing. If one assumes a pair of cuff links is one item, then the total equals 200 models. Also, in the NMAI inventory, the lids on cigarette boxes are listed as separate items. Spratling counted his cigarette boxes with lids as one item.

A full list of the 200 models that William Spratling provided as part of his contract is reproduced below. The letters and numbers in the captions to the photographs shown here relate directly to Spratling's list of the models.

One asterisk (*) indicates items missing from the NMAI collection.
Two asterisks (**) indicates items now in the Alaska State Museum.

Taxco-el-Viejo, Gro. Mexico
April 18, 1949

Article Cat. No.	Description	Material
Rings		
R-1	square-mounted (built-in) Kobuk jade, silver gilded.	
R-2	*one-piece mounted walrus ivory, 18K gold.	
R-3	*azurite, 18K gold.	
R-4	*azurite, baleen, silver.	
R-5	abalone, copper, baleen, silver.	
R-6	*triangular one-piece walrus ivory, inlaid 18K gold.	
R-7	*round one-piece walrus ivory, inlaid 18K gold.	
R-8	*azurite encrusted in silver, gilded.	
R-9	*one-piece ivory, baleen inlay, 18K. gold.	
R-10	*azurite segments in triangular silver.	
R-11	*Kobuk jade in silver, gilded.	
R-12	*ivory, baleen, in triangular silver.	
Earrings		
E-13	*walrus ivory tusk, silver, gilded.	
E-14	*gold loop, transparent ivory pendant ball, 18K gold.	
E-15	Kobuk jade in silver, gilded.	
E-16	thin star, carved beveled ivory, 18K gold (with N-116).	
E-17	segmented thin ivory disks, 18K gold ribs, star.	
E-18	carved fossil ivory, triple braid, 18K gold.	

Cufflinks

CL-19	polished baleen disk, encrusted star, silver.
CL-20	polished baleen square with ivory, 18K gold.
CL-21	baleen-ivory mosaic, 18K gold.
CL-22	miniature carved ivory walrus, polished baleen, 18K gold.
CL-23	square azurite mosaic, silver star incrusted.
CL-24	ivory walrus tusk, silver, gilded.

Buckles

BU-25	crossed walrus tusks, ivory, silver, gilded.
BU-26	inlaid compass in baleen, ivory, silver.
BU-27	small oval walrus tusks, ivory, silver, gilded.
BU-28	ivory, baleen arrows, deep inlay in silver.
BU-29	large Kobuk jade for women, silver, gilded.
BU-30	fossil ivory, baleen, inlaid in silver.
BU-31	white ivory, baleen, inlaid in silver.
BU-32	ivory and silver cord design, silver, gilded.
BU-33	fossil ivory, baleen, mounted with studs on silver.
BU-34	small walrus tusks, ivory, silver.

Buttons

BN-35-40	small triangular ivory star, triple binding, silver.
BN-41-46	medium triangular ivory star, triple binding, silver.
BN-47-52	hole carved ivory knot, silver, corded.
BN-53-58	hole carved ivory knot, hexagon, silver corded.
BN-59-64	square-carved fossil ivory, silver binding.
BN-65-70	large ivory claw, silver binding.
BN-71-76	small ivory claw, silver binding.
BN-77-82	medium ivory claw, silver binding.
BN-83-88	small baleen, ivory starred, silver banded.
BN-89-94	medium baleen, ivory starred, silver banded.
BN-95-100	carved mammoth ivory braided knot, silver gilded.
BN-101	large baleen disk, ivory starred inlay, silver banded.
BN-198-200	large ivory disk, silver star, silver banded.

Cigarette Boxes

CB-102	*primitive hand (right) fossil ivory mosaic, in silver repoussé, gilded.
CB-103	primitive hand (left) fossil ivory mosaic, in silver repoussé, gilded.
CB-104	**flag of Alaska, lapis lazuli turquoise mosaic, silver.
CB-105	*compass – north star, ivory baleen inlay, silver repoussé.
CB-106	transparent ivory paneled top, silver.
CB-107	*Tlingit eye, ivory, baleen, silver, gilded.

Pill Boxes

PB-108	compass – north star, ivory baleen inlay, silver repoussé.
PB-109	polar bear button (Muktoyuk) on hexagon, silver.
PB-110	*Eskimo face inlay, baleen, ivory, silver.

Necklaces and Collars

N-111	carved fossil ivory, triple braid, flexible, 18K gold.
N-112	walrus ivory cylindrical beads, claws, 18K gold disks.
N-113	*carved ivory shell, 18K gold.
N-114	mammoth ivory carved links, 18K gold.
N-115	*Eskimo ivory needles banded beaded, 18K gold.
N-116	carved – beveled gold - ivory star pendant, 18K beads.
N-117	heavy silver chain, carved S.E. Alaska abalone.
N-118	*Tlingit bear mask, abalone, baleen, silver repoussé.

Pendants and Lockets

PE-119 *beveled fossil ivory, secret panel, 18K gold.
PE-120 carved transparent fossil ivory, hinged, silver, gilded.
PE-121 paneled compass – north star, baleen, fossil ivory, 18K.
PE-122 *forty-niner star, fossil ivory mosaic, 18K gold.
PE-123 *Tlingit mask, profile, carved silver, abalone.
PE-124 pendant.

Pins

PN-125 carved fossil ivory, triple braid, 18K gold (with N-111).
PN-126 pendant badge, carved ivory gold panels, 18K gold.
PN-127 the four winds, mammoth ivory, baleen center, 18K gold.

Crosses

CR-128 large, one piece Kobuk jade, silver, gilded.
CR-129 *inlaid fossil ivory, 18K gold.

Bracelets

BR-130 *fossil ivory graduated with large beads, 18K gold.
BR-131 white ivory with silver, gilded, corded design.
BR-132 mammoth ivory carved links, 18K gold (with N-114).
BR-133 *polar bear fangs on hollow silver, gilded.
BR-134 *inlaid white and fossil ivory, silver, gilded.
BR-135 *inlaid tones of fossil ivory, silver, gilded.
BR-136 carved ivory, hinged, silver, gilded (triple braid).

Candlesticks

CS-137 low, fossil ivory base turned, silver, gilded.
CS-138 low, fossil ivory base turned, silver.

Cups and Goblets

CU-139 jigger, carved malachite hand base, silver.
CU-140 jigger, carved ivory hand base, silver, gilded.
CU-141-146 brandy, turned ivory base, silver (6 pcs).
CU-147 goblet, ivory base and column, spiral, silver.
CU-192-197 liquor, lapis lazuli base, silver (6 pcs).

Knives

Pocket

PK-148 rebuilt hunting, Kobuk jade in silver, gilt handle.

Serving

SK-149 steak, ivory-baleen arrow inlay handle, stainless blade.

Meat

MK-150 steak, baleen-ivory handle, stainless steel blade.
MK-151 carving, carved fossil ivory, mountain sheep, stainless.

Fruit

FK-152 ivory-baleen arrow inlay, stainless steel.

Butter

BK-153 fossil ivory, silver inlay, stainless steel.
BK-154 baleen, ivory inlay, stainless steel.

Letter Openers

PC-155 Tlingit bird head handle, garnet eye inset from Wrangell, carved silver (not cast).

Paper Cutters

PC-156 cord-motive, ivory blade, silver handle.
PC-157 walrus head, ivory-baleen, silver blade.
PC-158 *primitive spear-head, carved mammoth ivory, spiral column, silver.
PC-159 Tlingit raven, chiseled silver, ivory inlay.
PC-160 *Tlingit raven, chiseled silver, abalone inlay.
PC-161 Kobuk jade, inlaid, silver, gilded.

Spoons

Salt

SS-162-167 silver-arrow-on-ivory inset, silver.

Tea

TS-168-173 silver-arrow-on-ivory inset, silver.

Serving

SV-174 transparent inlay, baleen arrow, ivory, silver.

Salad

SA-175 fossil ivory whale handle, hammered silver.

Pastry spatula

PS-176 transparent inlay, baleen arrow, ivory, silver.

Sugar

SS-177 Tlingit raven spoon, abalone mounting, silver.

Forks

Salad

SF-178 fossil ivory whale handle, hammered silver.

Meat

MF-179 carved fossil ivory, mountain sheep.

Ashtrays

AT-180 hexagonal, bear-tooth base, silver.
AT-181 one-piece low, 3-claw, fossil ivory base, silver.
AT-182 one-piece low, 3-claw, fossil ivory base.
AT-183 low square, heavy silver, gilded, four feet, Kobuk jade.
AT-184 low triangular, heavy silver, gilded, three feet, Kobuk jade.

Cigarette Holders

CH-185 long ivory, inlay of 18K gold disks.
CH-186 long ivory, inlay of 18K gold arrows.
CH-187 *small, fluted fossil ivory, 18K gold bindings.

Bonbon Nuts

BB-188 **Tlingit motive (shape), ivory base, silver, gilded.
BB-189 Tlingit motive corded, ivory base, silver.

Bells

BL-190 carved and lacquered silver, early walrus-whale hunt motifs, spouting whale handle of carved and turned fossil ivory.

Paperweight

PW-191 sculptured "Moby Dick," mammoth ivory on Kobuk jade and heavy silver base.

Of the original two hundred models produced by Spratling by 1949, one hundred sixty-eight are at the National Museum of American Indian's Cultural Resource Center. Only thirty-two pieces are missing from their inventory. With two separate items from the original project at Alaska's State Museum, that leaves only thirty missing pieces. The missing items include bracelets, rings, necklaces and earrings.

Photographs of thirty models in the possession of the National Museum of the American Indian are included herein, along with Spratling's original design drawings for these models. These original drawings for the models were found at the offices of Sucesores de Wm Spratling in Mexico City, with the assistance of Violante Ulrich and Consuelo Ulrich, Some of these original drawings include William Spratling's notations regarding the actual model numbers.

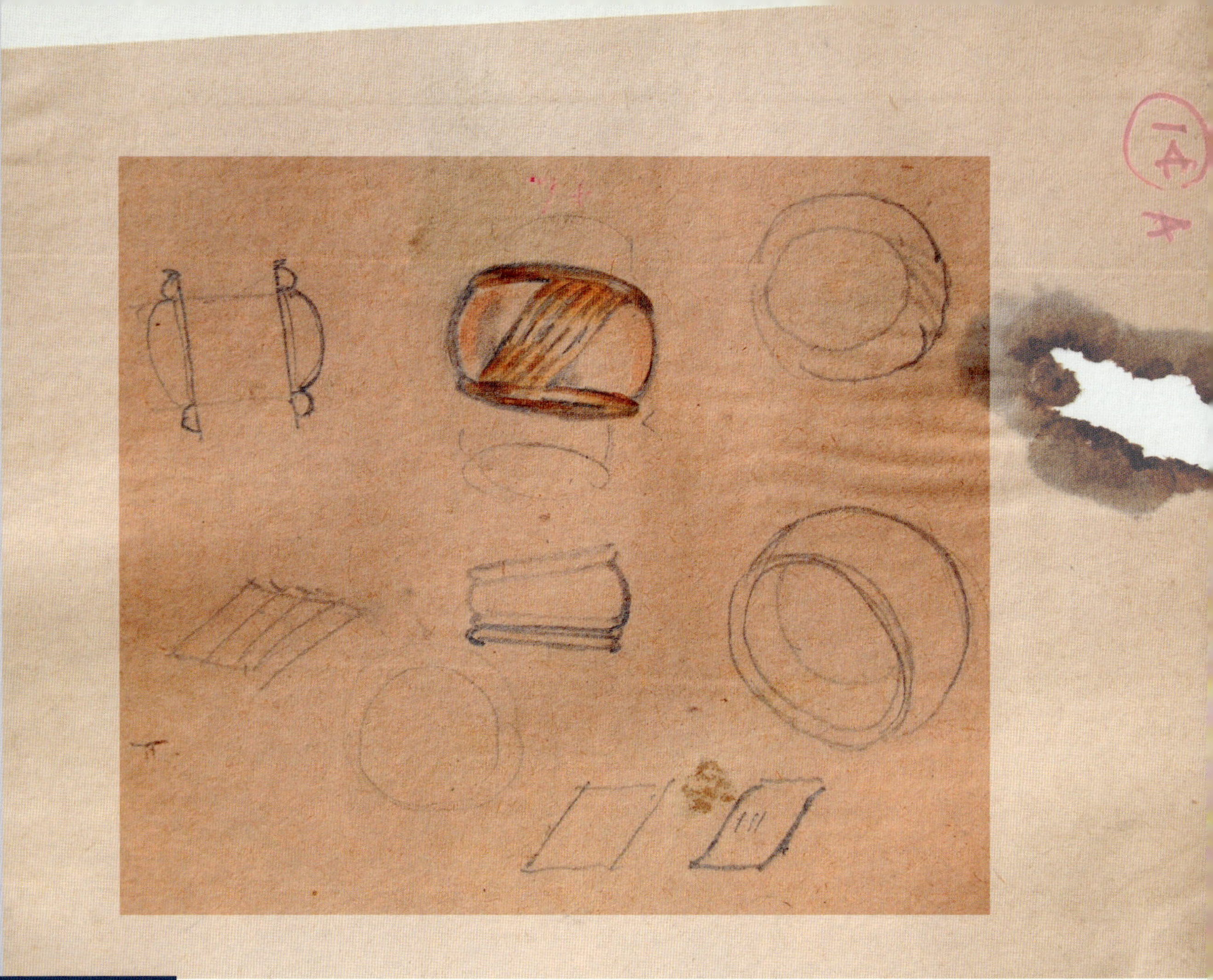

R 4, similar to R 5. Original design drawing. Courtesy of Sucesores de Wm Spratling, S.A. de C.V.

Rings

R 5. Ring, abalone, copper, baleen, silver. Courtesy, National Museum of the American Indian, Smithsonian Institution

E 18. Earrings, carved fossil ivory, triple braid, 18K gold. Courtesy, National Museum of the American Indian, Smithsonian Institution

EARRINGS

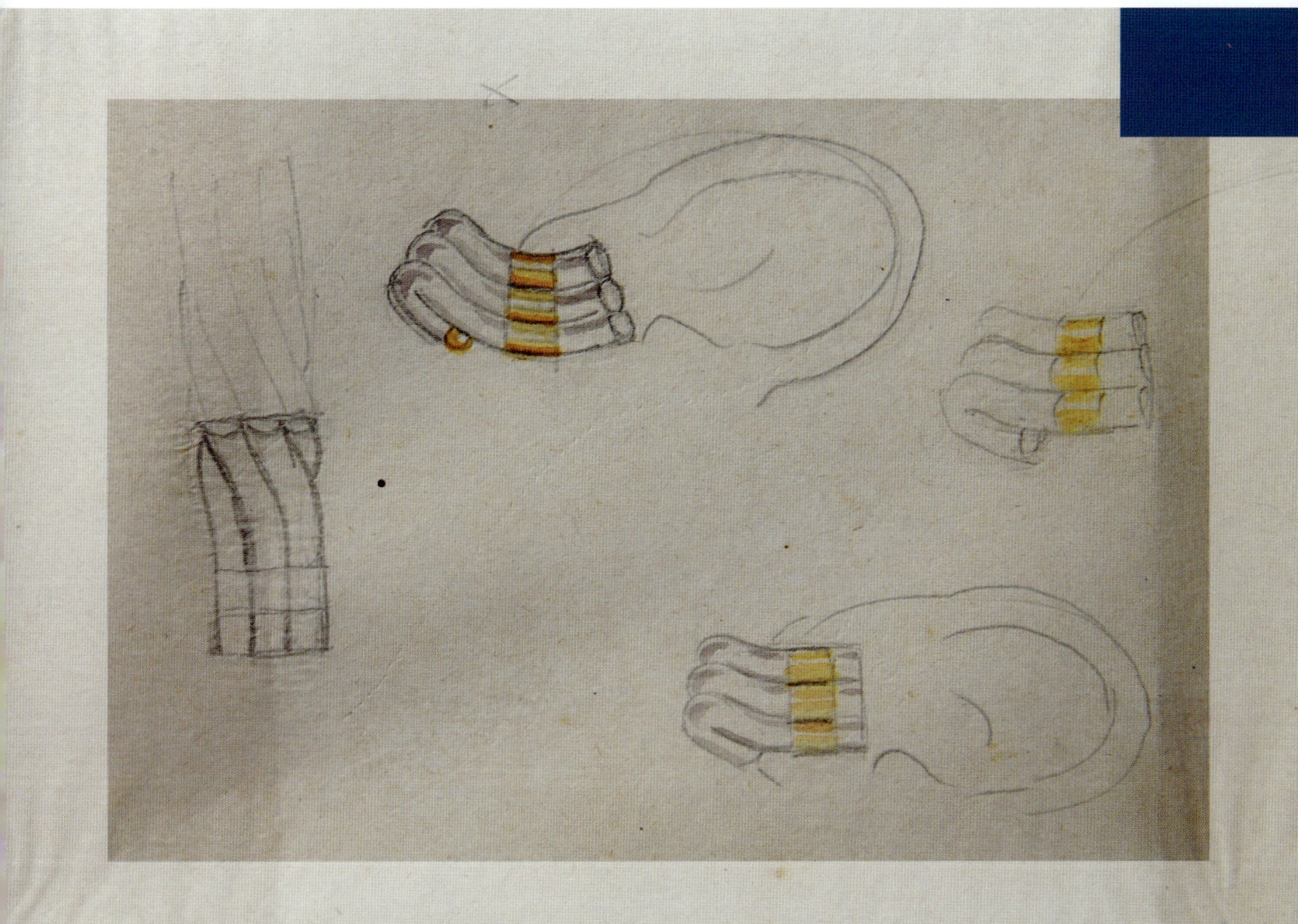

E 18. Original design drawing. Courtesy of Sucesores de Wm Spratling, S.A. de C.V.

CL 19. Original design drawings. Courtesy of Sucesores de Wm Spratling, S.A. de C.V.

Cufflinks

CL 19. Cufflinks, polished baleen disk, incrusted silver star, silver. Courtesy, National Museum of the American Indian, Smithsonian Institution

CL 23. Cufflinks, square azurite mosaic, silver star encrusted. Courtesy, National Museum of the American Indian, Smithsonian Institution

CL21. Cufflinks, baleen-ivory mosaic, 18K gold. Courtesy, National Museum of the American Indian, Smithsonian Institution

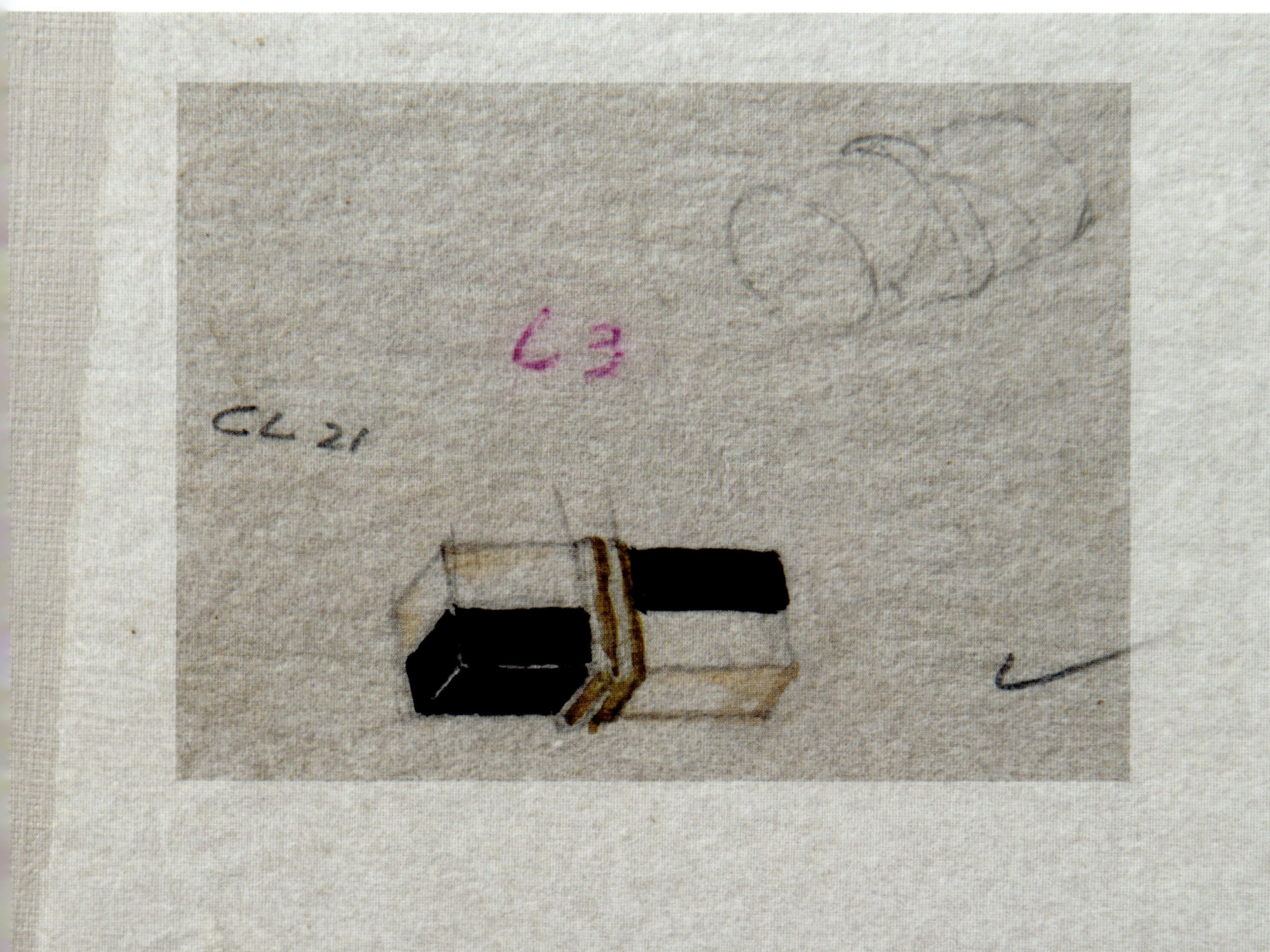

CL 21. Original design drawing. Courtesy of Sucesores de Wm Spratling, S.A. de C.V.

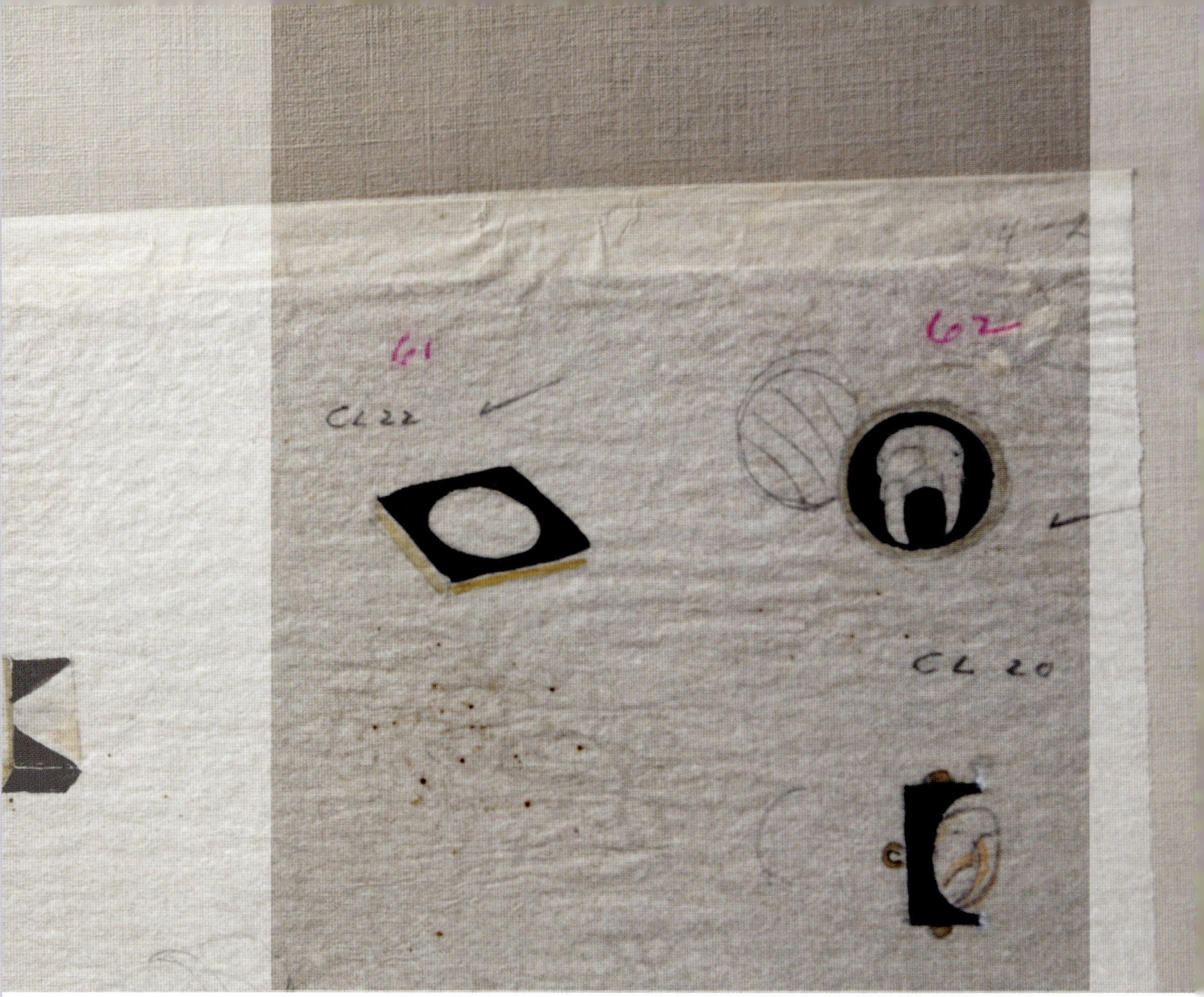

CL 20. Original design drawings. Courtesy of Sucesores de Wm Spratling, S.A. de C.V.

CL 22. Original design drawing. Courtesy of Sucesores de Wm Spratling, S.A. de C.V.

CL 22. Cufflinks, miniature carved ivory walrus, polished baleen, 18K gold. Courtesy, National Museum of the American Indian, Smithsonian Institution

CL 20. Cufflinks, polished baleen square with ivory, 18K gold. Courtesy, National Museum of the American Indian, Smithsonian Institution

CL 24. Cufflinks, ivory walrus tusk, silver, gilded. Courtesy, National Museum of the American Indian, Smithsonian Institution

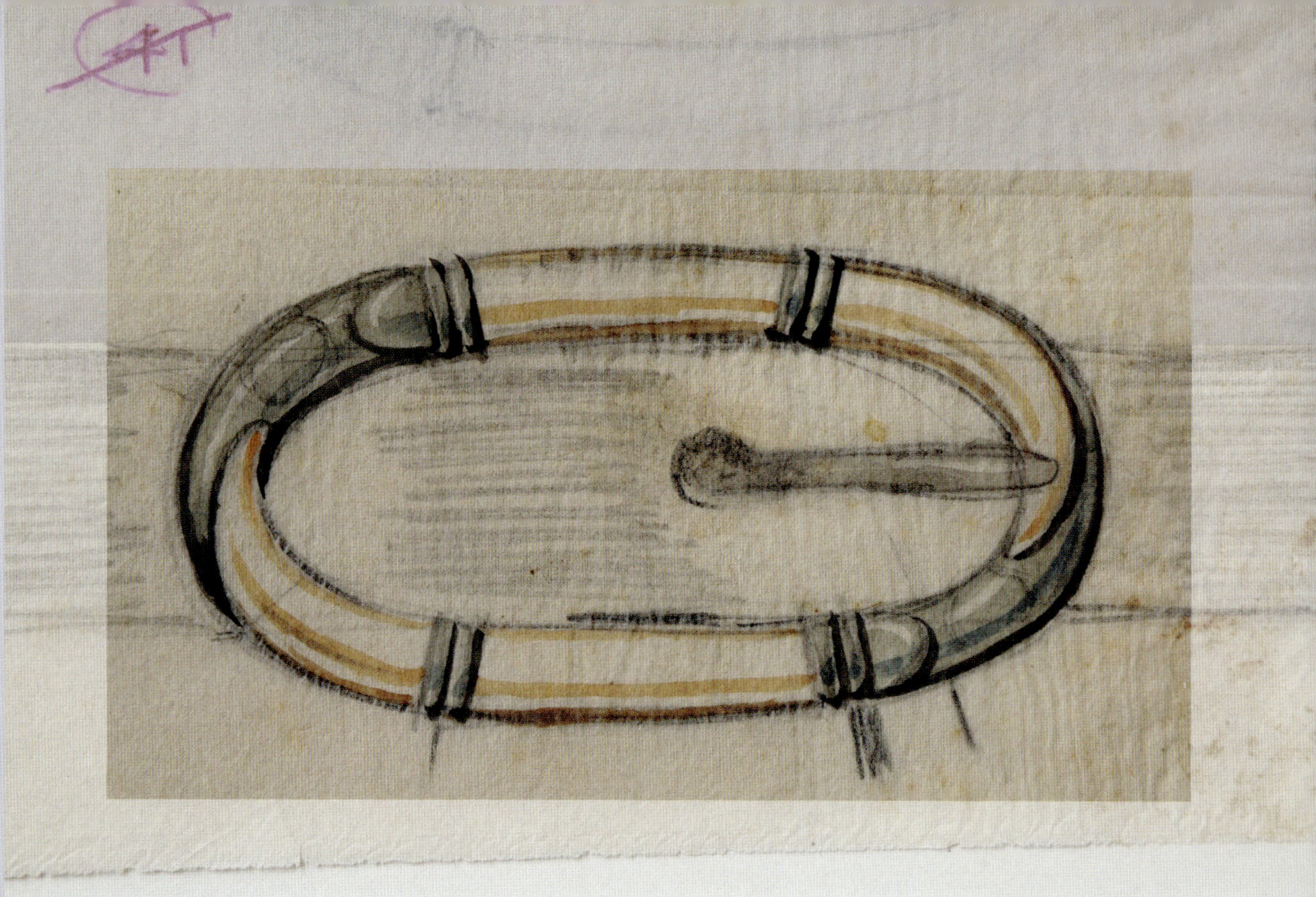

BU 25. Original design drawing. Courtesy of Sucesores de Wm Spratling, S.A. de C.V.

BUCKLES

BU 25. Buckle, crossed walrus tusks, ivory, silver, gilded. Courtesy, National Museum of the American Indian, Smithsonian Institution

BU 29. Buckle, large Kobuk jade for women, silver, gilded. Courtesy, National Museum of the American Indian, Smithsonian Institution

BU 29. Original design drawing. Courtesy of Sucesores de Wm Spratling, S.A. de C.V.

BU 26. Buckle, inlaid compass design in baleen, ivory, silver. Courtesy, National Museum of the American Indian, Smithsonian Institution

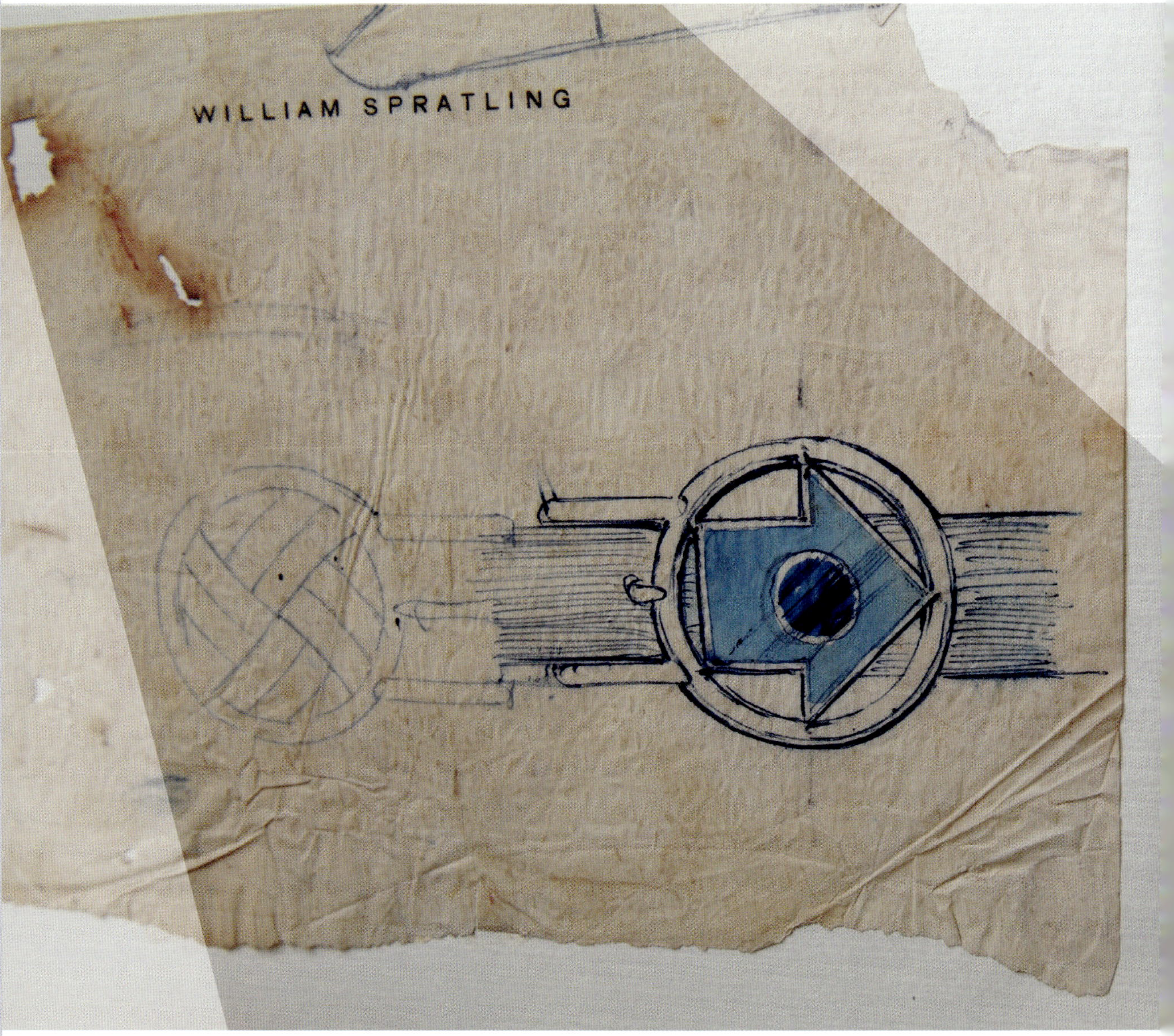

* BU An original design drawing for a belt buckle. **Buckle missing.** Courtesy of Sucesores de Wm Spratling, S.A. de C.V.

BU 30. Original design drawing. Courtesy of Sucesores de Wm Spratling, S.A. de C.V.

BU 30. Buckle, fossil ivory, baleen, inlaid in silver. Courtesy, National Museum of the American Indian, Smithsonian Institution

* Original design drawings for buttons and cufflinks. Missing is a set of earrings. Courtesy of Sucesores de Wm Spratling, S.A. de C.V.

BUTTONS

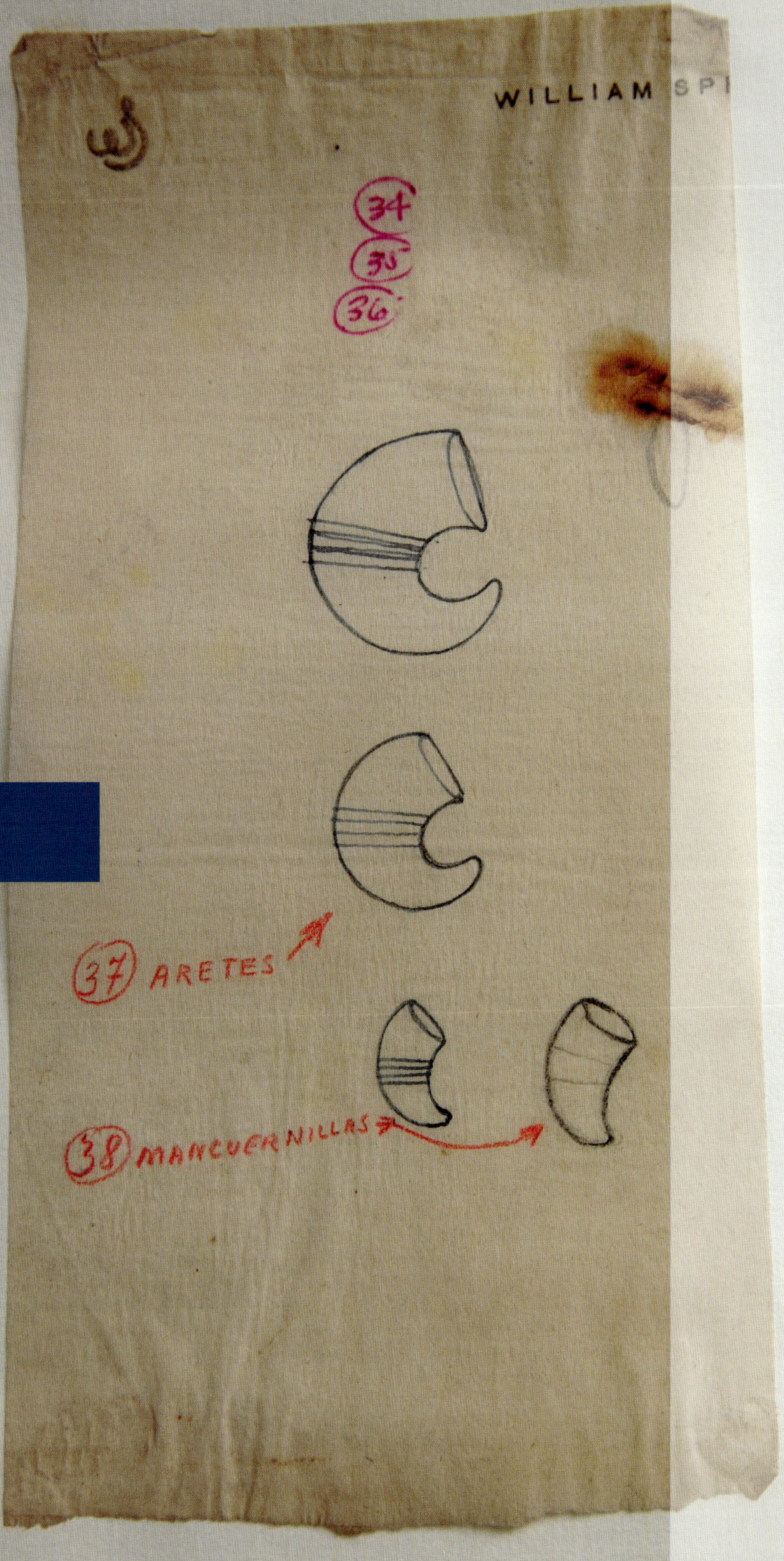

BN 65-70. Large ivory claw, silver binding. Courtesy, National Museum of the American Indian, Smithsonian Institution

BN 71-76. Buttons, small ivory claw, silver binding. Courtesy, National Museum of the American Indian, Smithsonian Institution

* BN 77-82. Buttons, medium ivory claw, silver binding. **One of the original six is missing**. Courtesy, National Museum of the American Indian, Smithsonian Institution

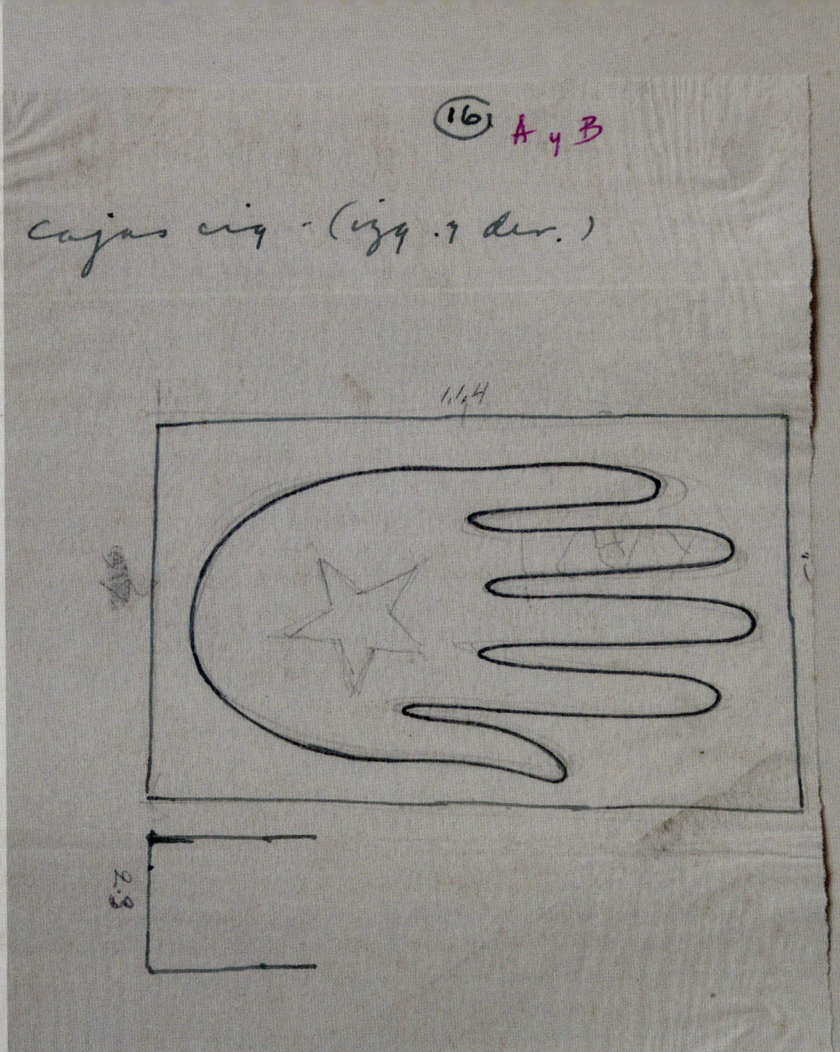

CB 103. Original design drawing. Courtesy of Sucesores de Wm Spratling, S.A. de C.V.

Cigarette Boxes

CB 103. Cigarette box, primitive hand (left) fossil ivory mosaic, in silver repoussé gilded. Courtesy, National Museum of the American Indian, Smithsonian Institution

PB 107. Pill box, Tlingit eye of ivory, baleen, silver, gilded. Courtesy, National Museum of the American Indian, Smithsonian Institution

CB-106. Pill Box, ivory and silver. Courtesy, National Museum of the American Indian, Smithsonian Institution

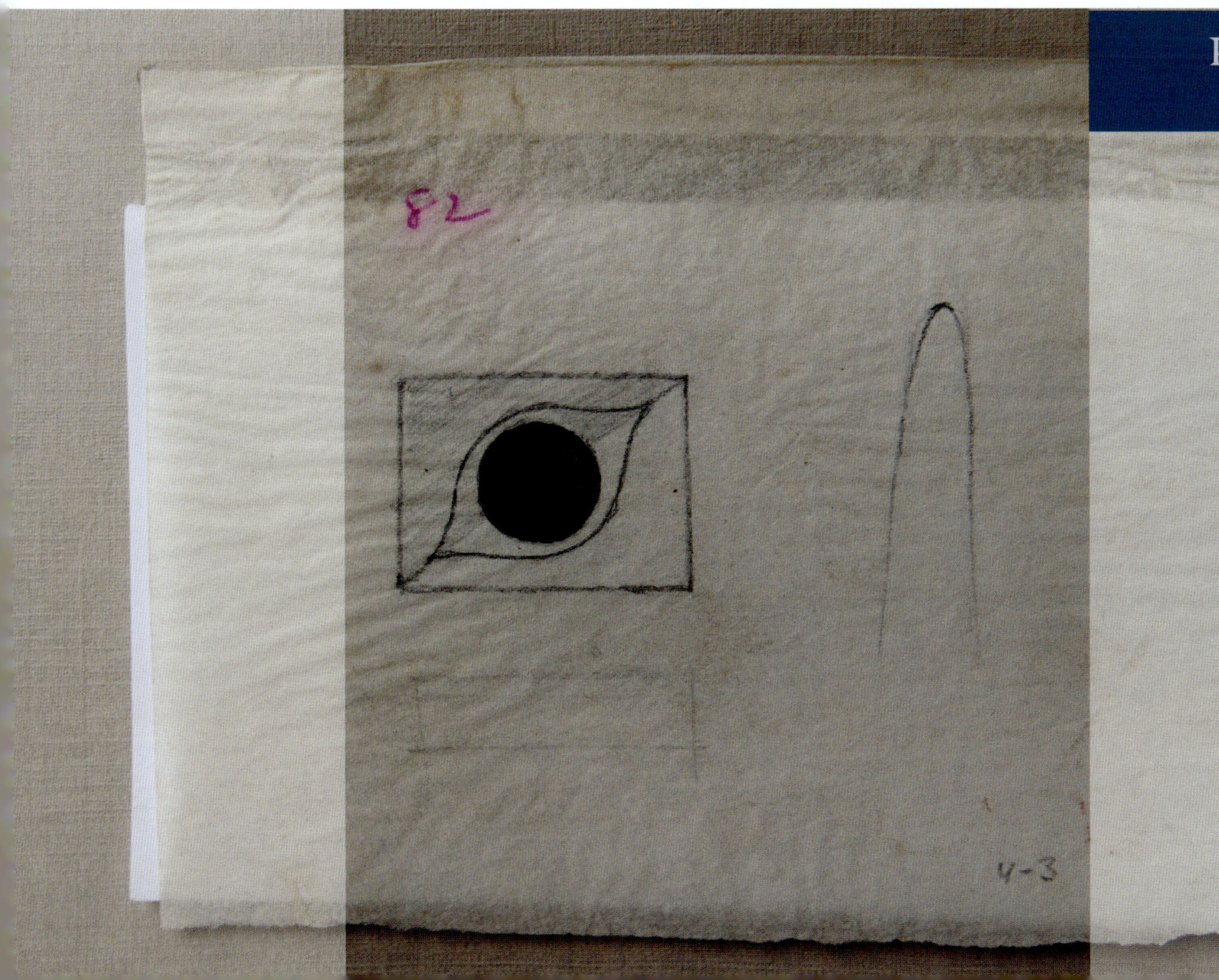

PB 107. Original design drawing. Courtesy of Sucesores de Wm Spratling, S.A. de C.V.

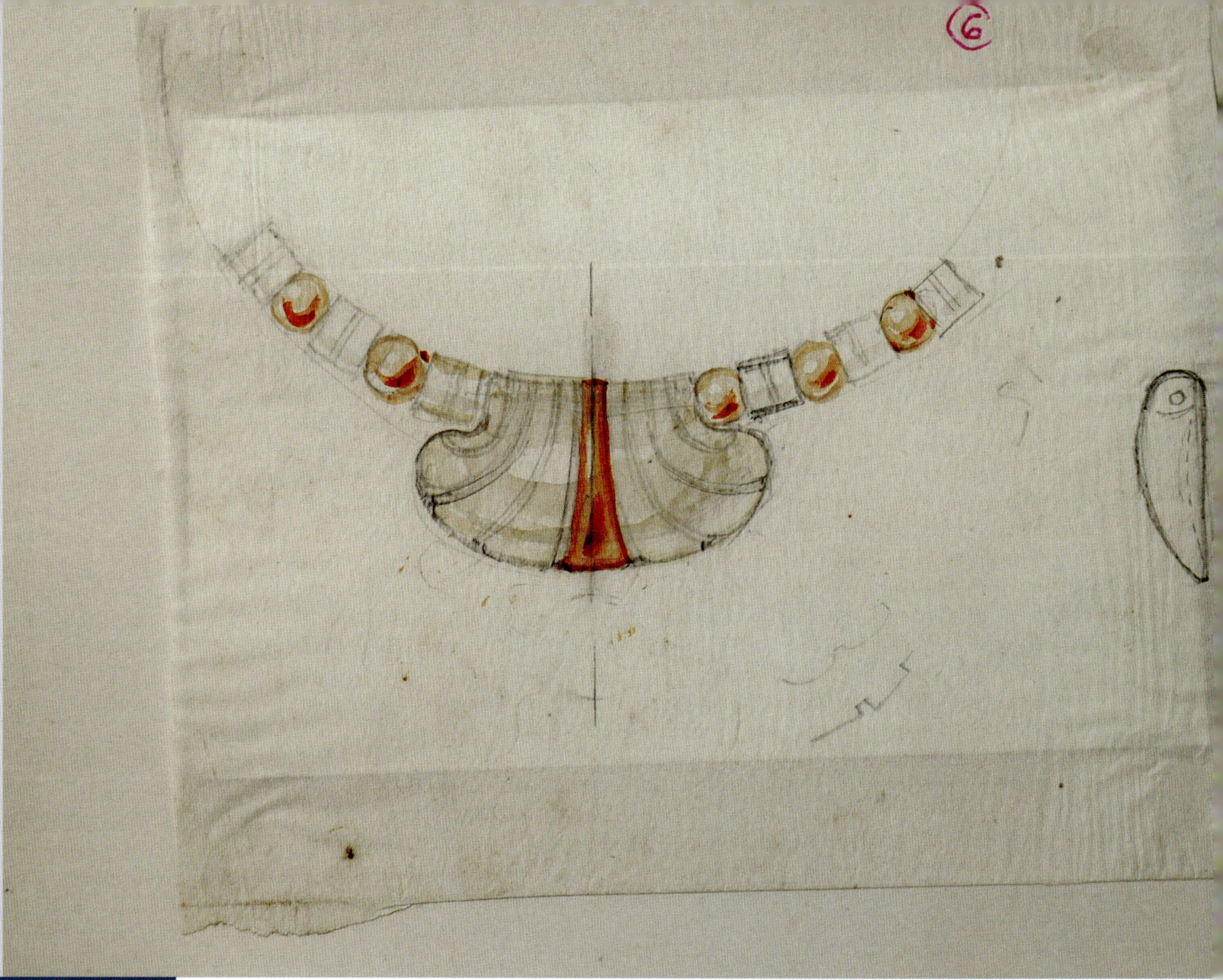

* N 113. Original design drawing. Necklace, carved ivory shell, 18K gold. **Necklace missing.** Courtesy of Sucesores de Wm Spratling, S.A. de C.V.

N 116. Original design drawing. Courtesy of Sucesores de Wm Spratling, S.A. de C.V.

N 117. Necklace, heavy silver chain, carved S.E. Alaska abalone. Courtesy, National Museum of the American Indian, Smithsonian Institution

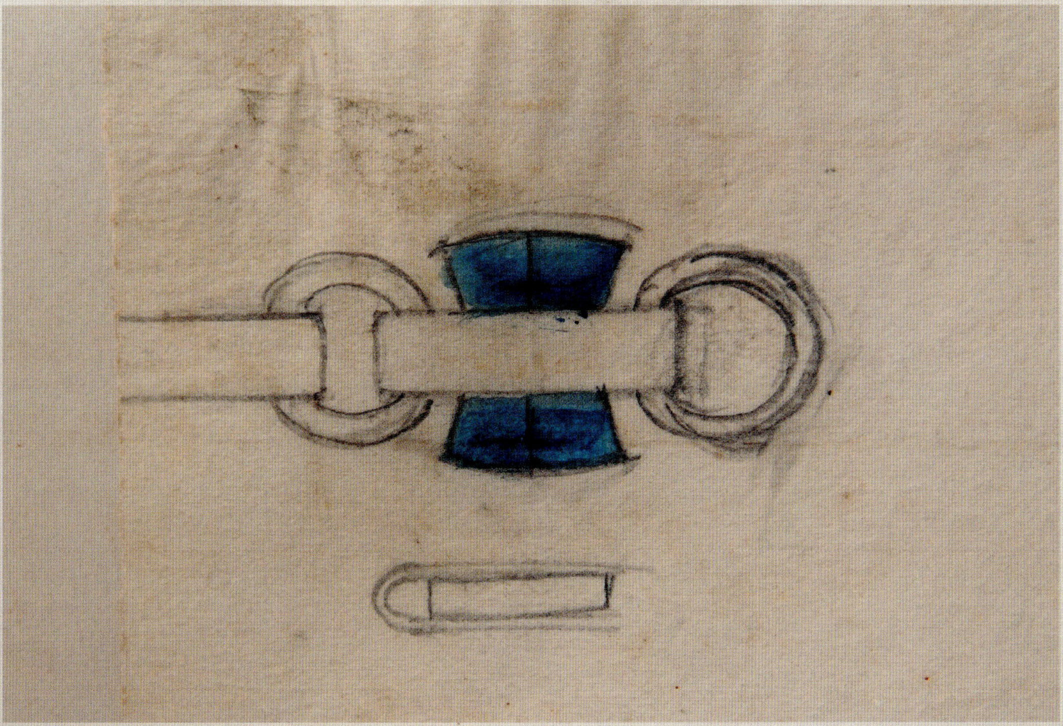

N 117. Original design drawings. Courtesy of Sucesores de Wm Spratling, S.A. de C.V.

N114 Necklace. mammoth ivory carved links, 18K gold. Courtesy, National Museum of the American Indian, Smithsonian Institution

N 114 and BR 132. Necklace and bracelet. Original design drawing. Courtesy of Sucesores de Wm Spratling, S.A. de C.V.

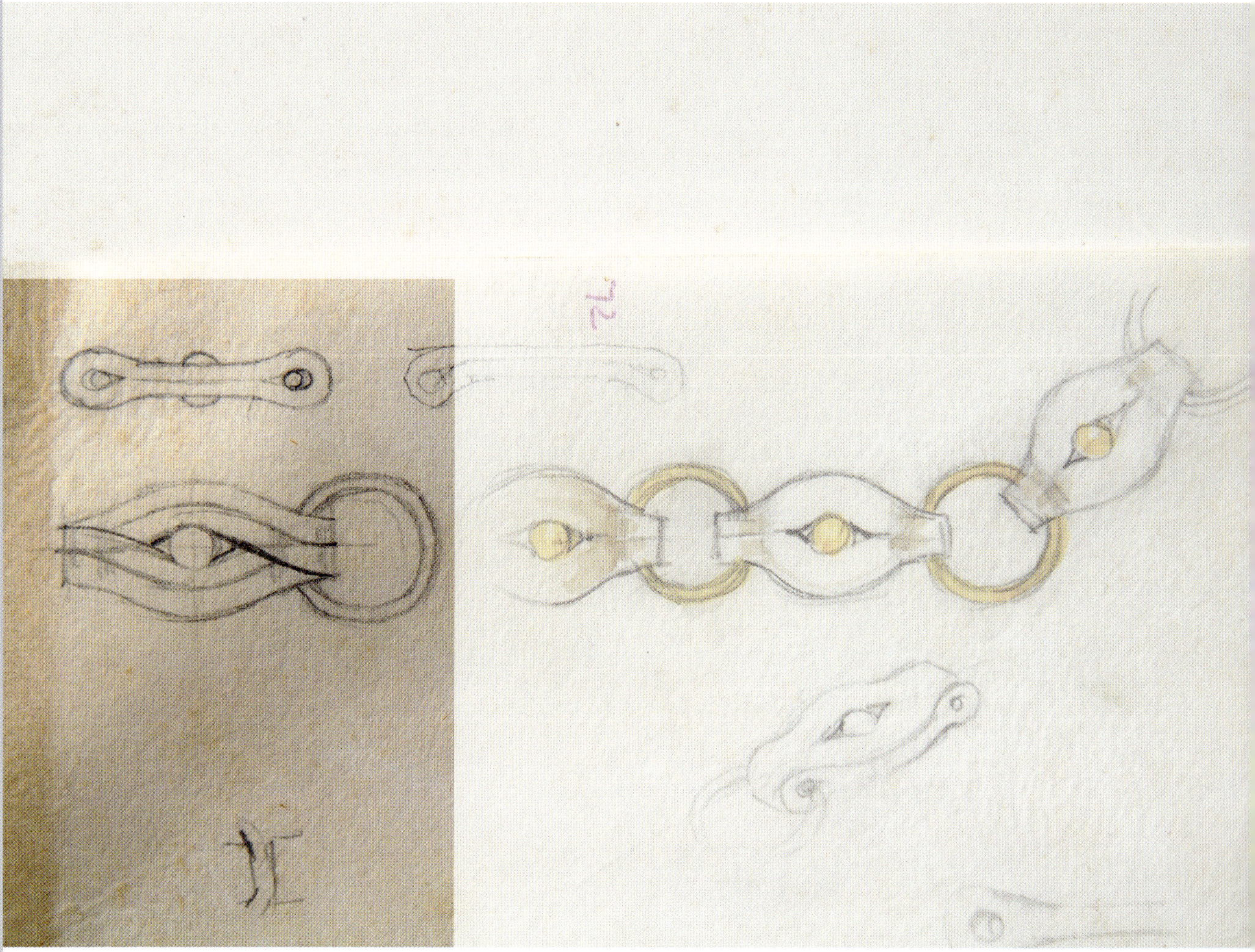

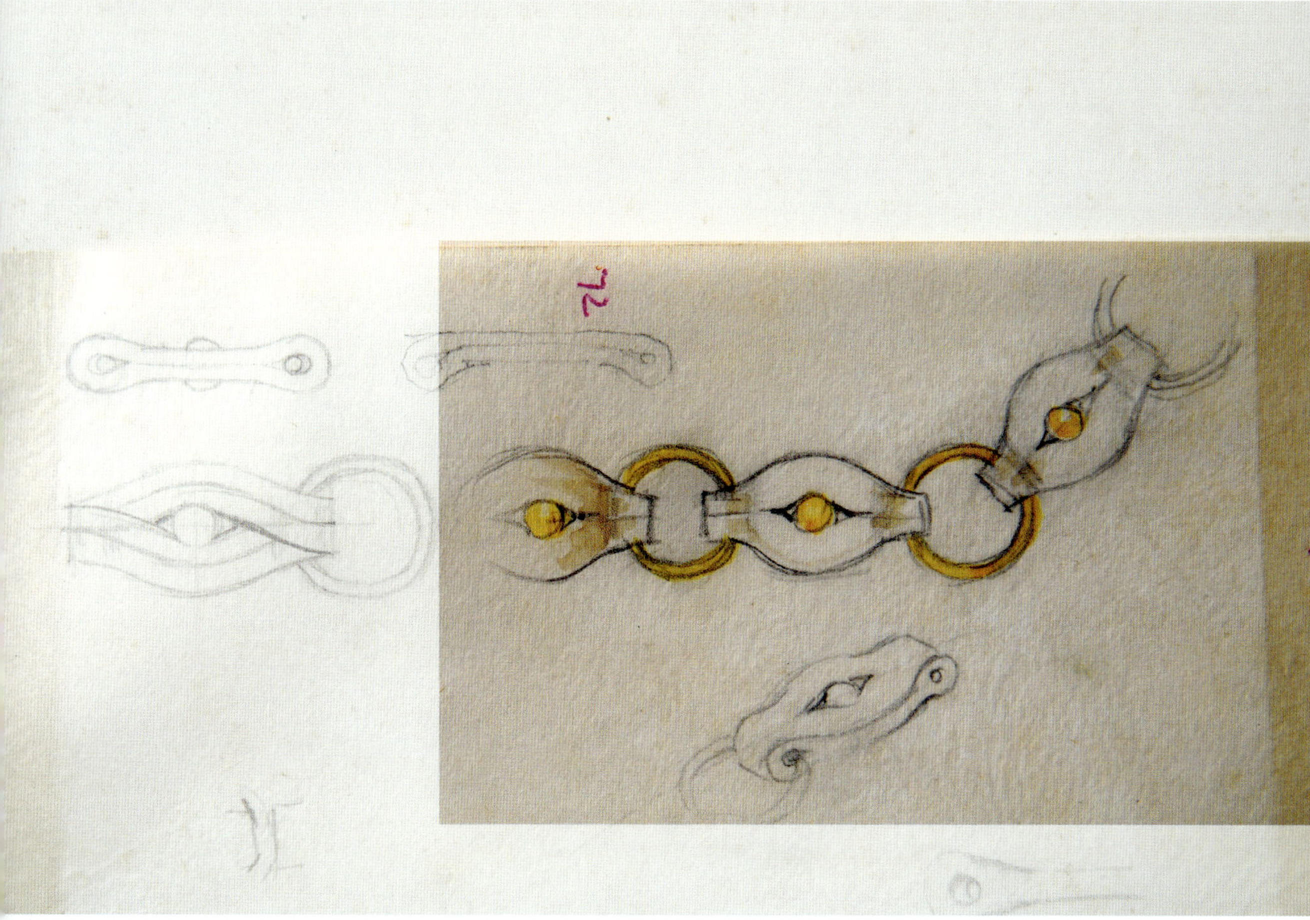

BRACELETS

BR 132. Bracelet, mammoth ivory carved links, 18K gold. Courtesy, National Museum of the American Indian, Smithsonian Institution

BR 131. Bracelet, white ivory with silver, gilded, corded design. Courtesy, National Museum of the American Indian, Smithsonian Institution

BR 131. Original design drawing. Courtesy of Sucesores de Wm Spratling, S.A. de C.V.

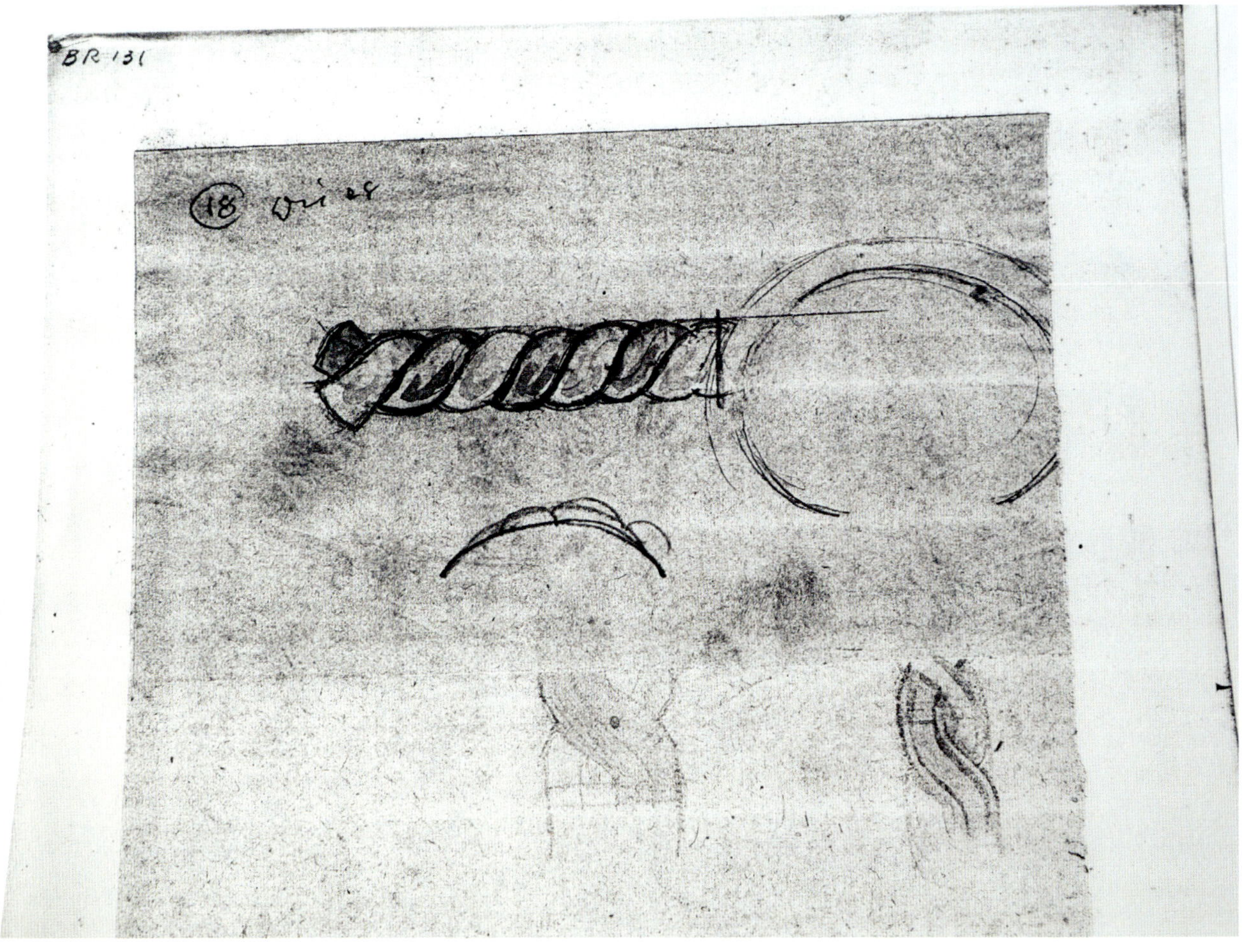

* BR 134 or 135. Original design drawing. Bracelet, inlaid white and fossil ivory, silver, gilded. **Bracelets missing.** Courtesy of Sucesores de Wm Spratling, S.A. de C.V.

PN 127. Original design drawing. Courtesy of Sucesores de Wm Spratling, S.A. de C.V.

PINS

PN 127. Pin indicating the four winds, mammoth ivory, baleen center, 18K gold. Courtesy, National Museum of the American Indian, Smithsonian Institution

* PE 123. Original design drawing. Pendant, Tlingit mask, profile, carved silver, abalone. **Pendant missing.** Courtesy of Sucesores de Wm Spratling, S.A. de C.V.

* PE 122. Original design drawing. Pendant, forty-niner star, fossil ivory mosaic, 18K gold. **Pendant missing.** Courtesy of Sucesores de Wm Spratling, S.A. de C.V.

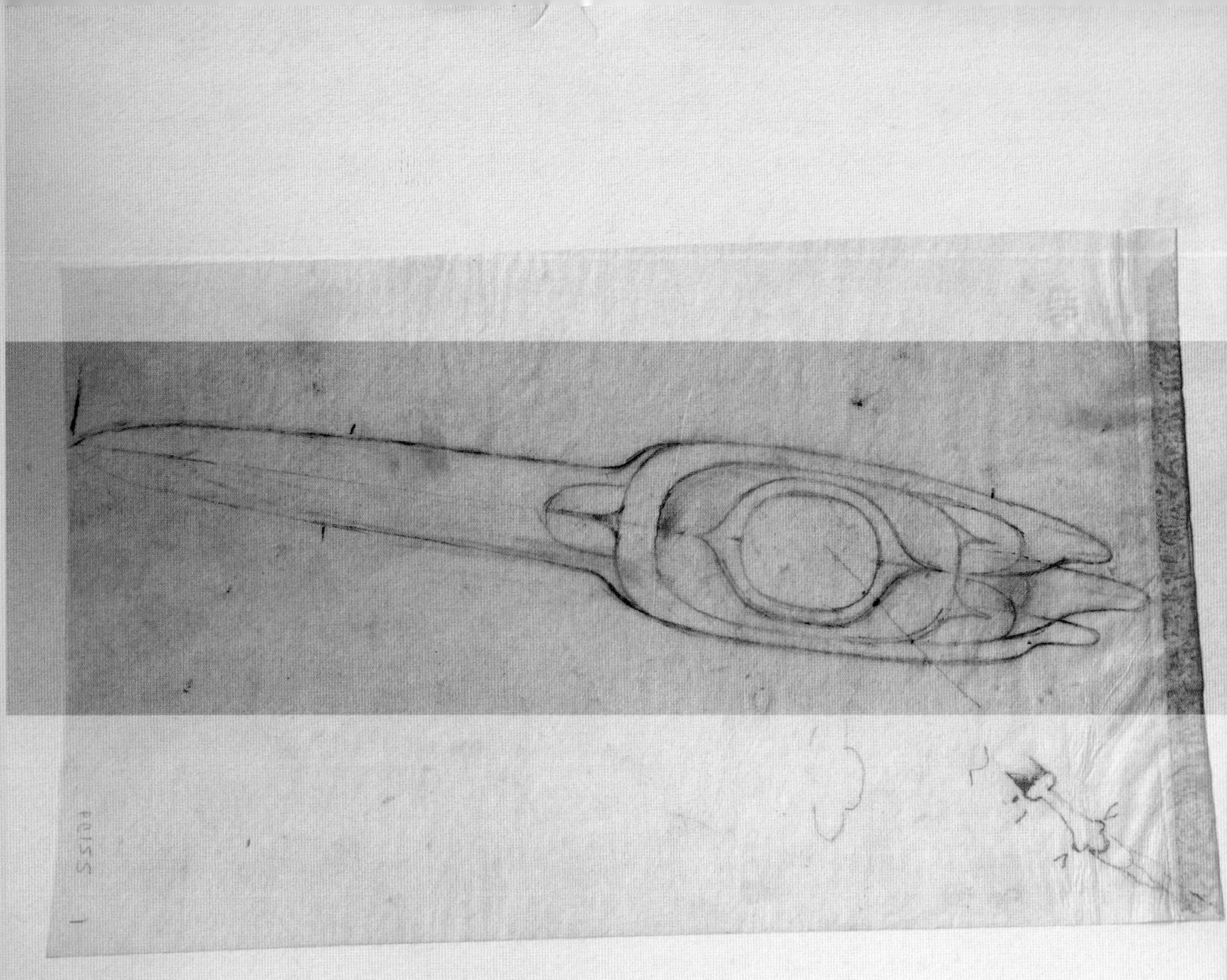

PC 155. Original design drawing. Courtesy of Sucesores de Wm Spratling, S.A. de C.V.

KNIVES

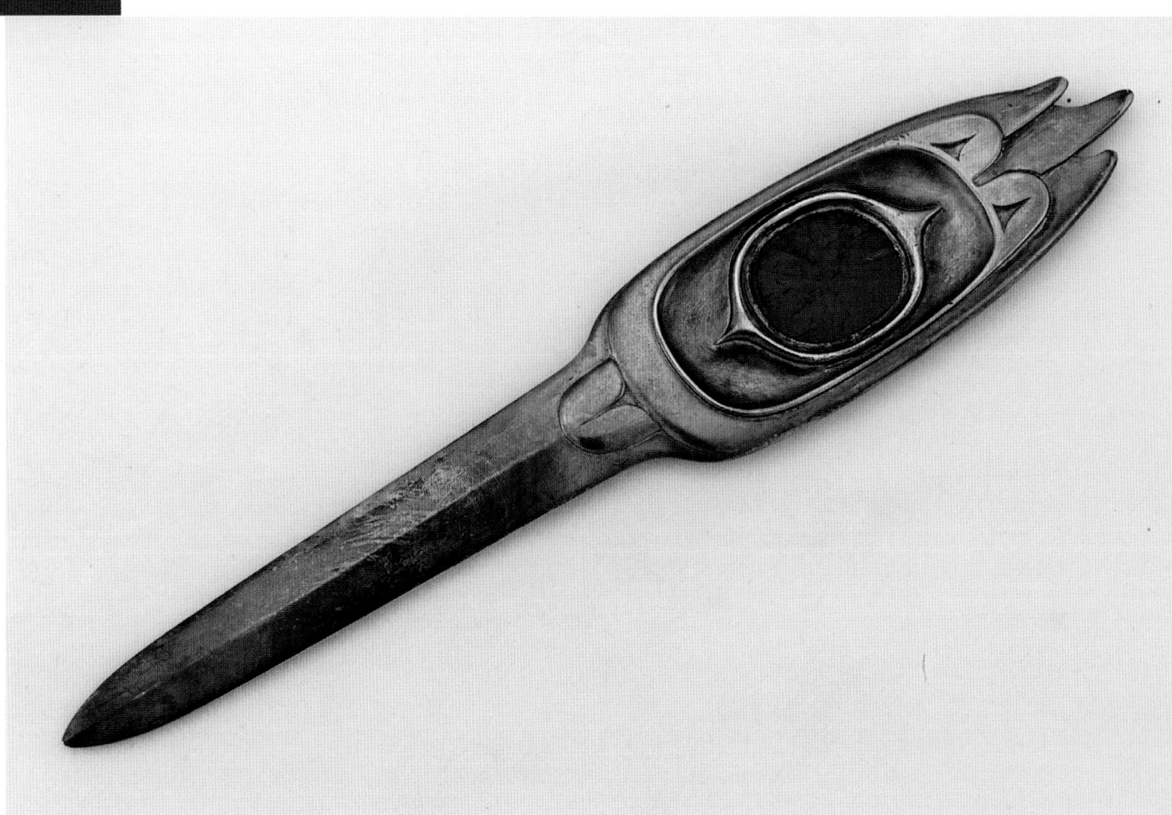

PC 155. Paper cutter, or letter opener, with Tlingit bird-head handle, garnet eye inset from Wrangell, carved silver (not cast). Courtesy, National Museum of the American Indian, Smithsonian Institution

PC 157. Paper cutter, walrus head, ivory-baleen, silver blade. Courtesy, National Museum of the American Indian, Smithsonian Institution

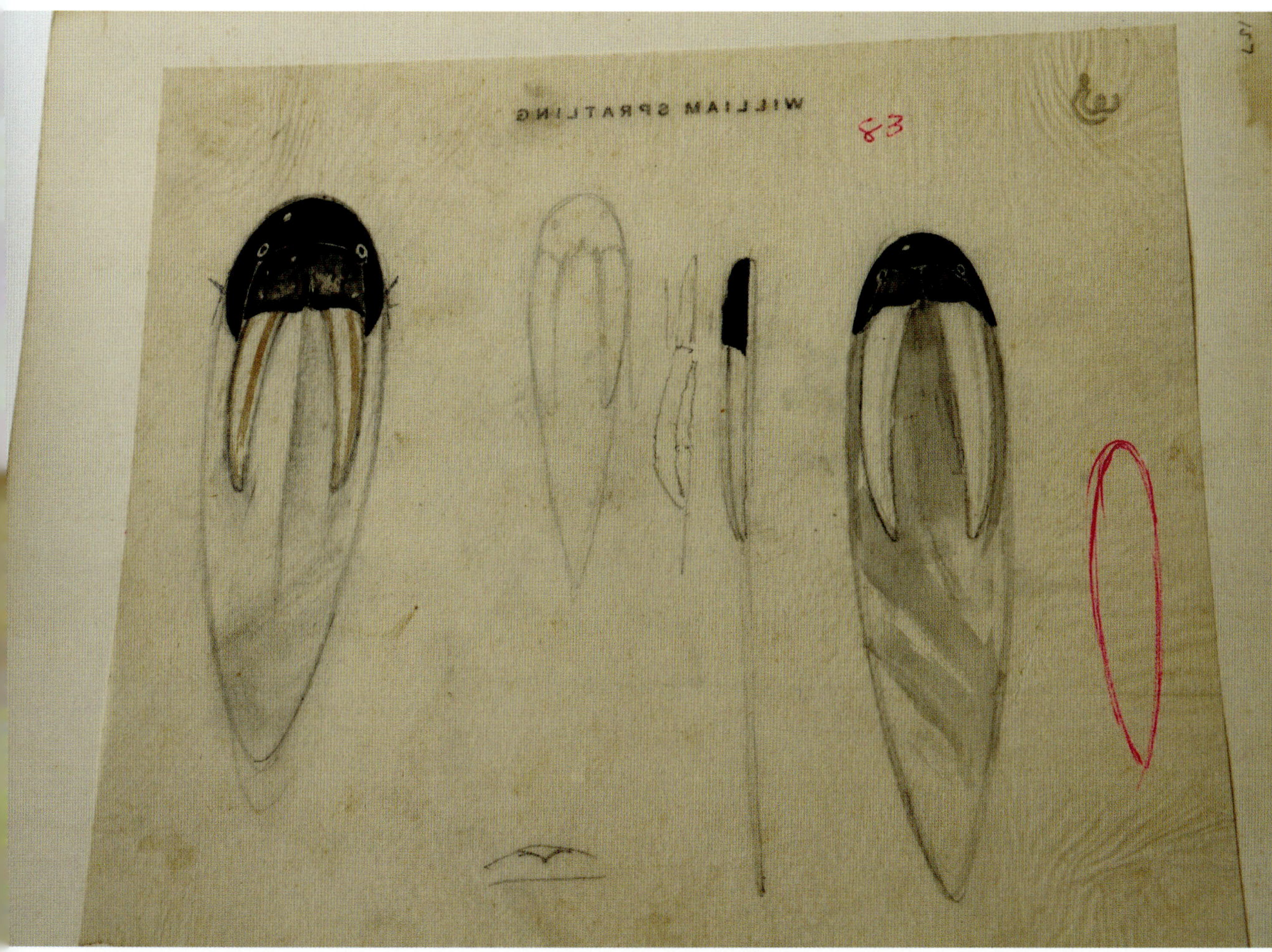

PC 157. Original design drawing. Courtesy of Sucesores de Wm Spratling, S.A. de C.V.

SV 174. Original design drawing. Courtesy of Sucesores de Wm Spratling, S.A. de C.V.

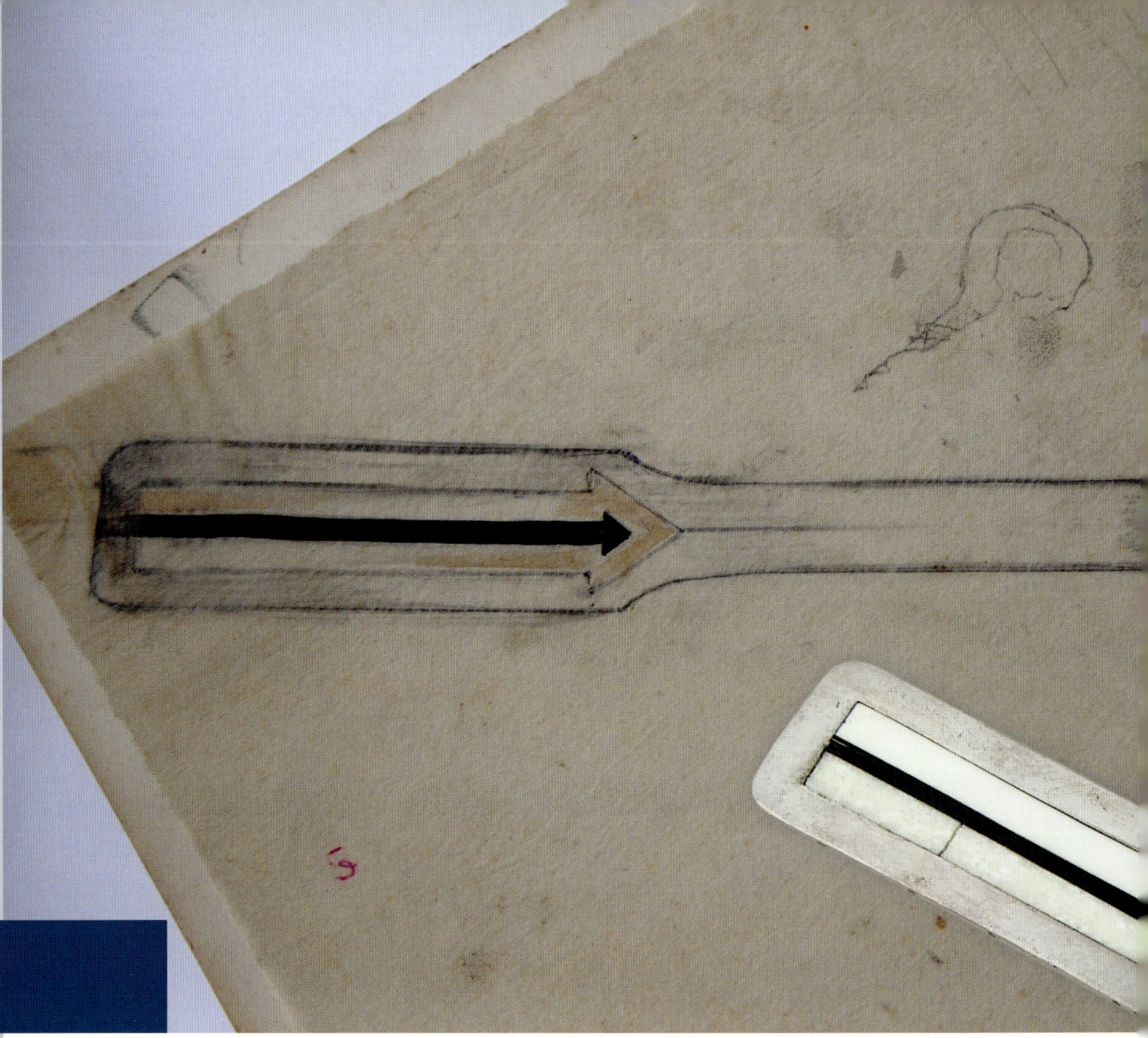

Spoons

TS 168-173. Tea spoons, silver-arrow-on-ivory inset, silver. Courtesy, National Museum of the American Indian, Smithsonian Institution

SV 174. Serving spoon, transparent inlay, baleen arrow, ivory, silver. Courtesy, National Museum of the American Indian, Smithsonian Institution

SS 162-167 and TS 168-173. Original design drawings. Courtesy of Sucesores de Wm Spratling, S.A. de C.V.

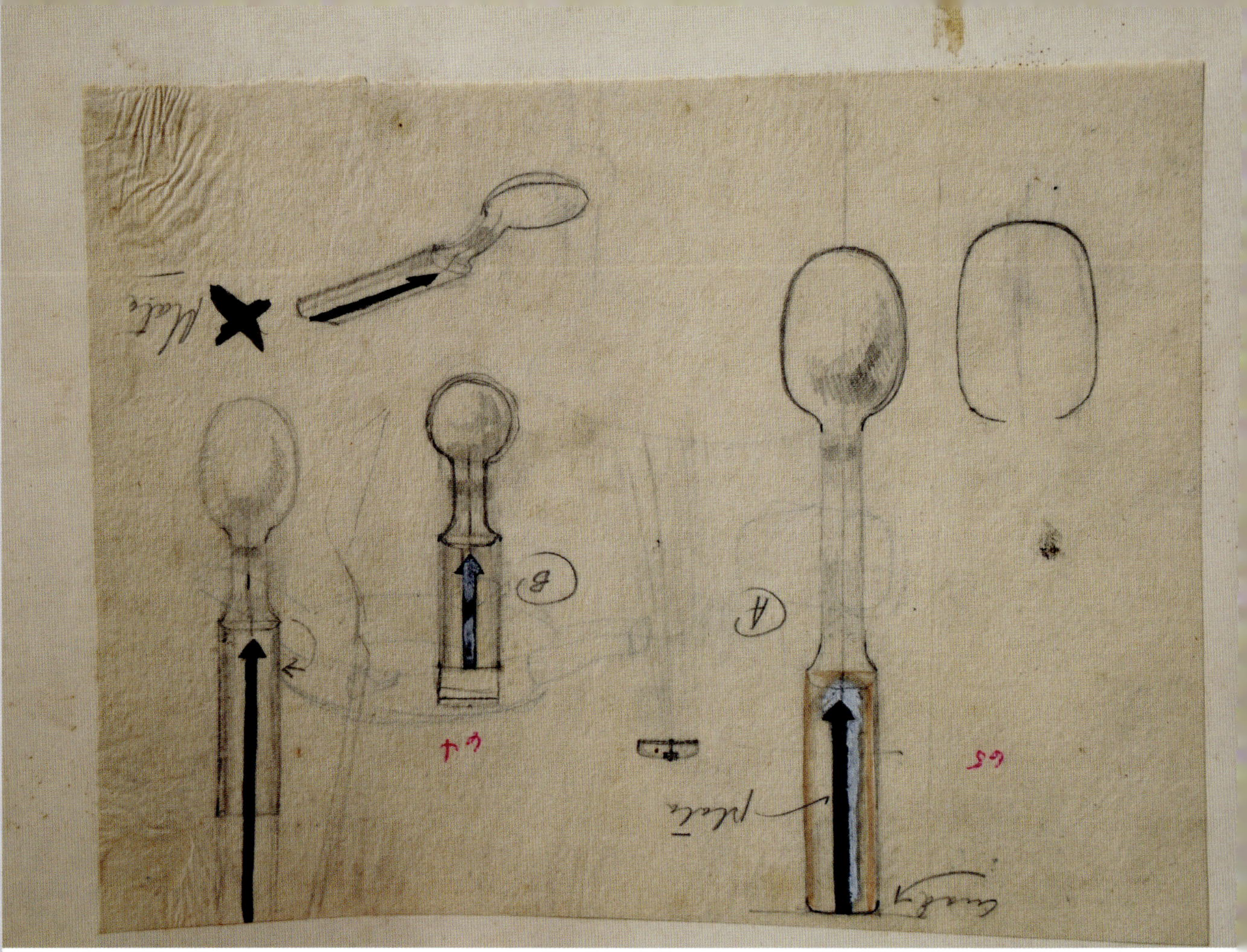

SS 162-167. Salt spoons, silver-arrow-on-ivory inset, silver. Courtesy, National Museum of the American Indian, Smithsonian Institution

PS 176. Pastry spoon, transparent inlay, baleen arrow, ivory, silver. Courtesy, National Museum of the American Indian, Smithsonian Institution

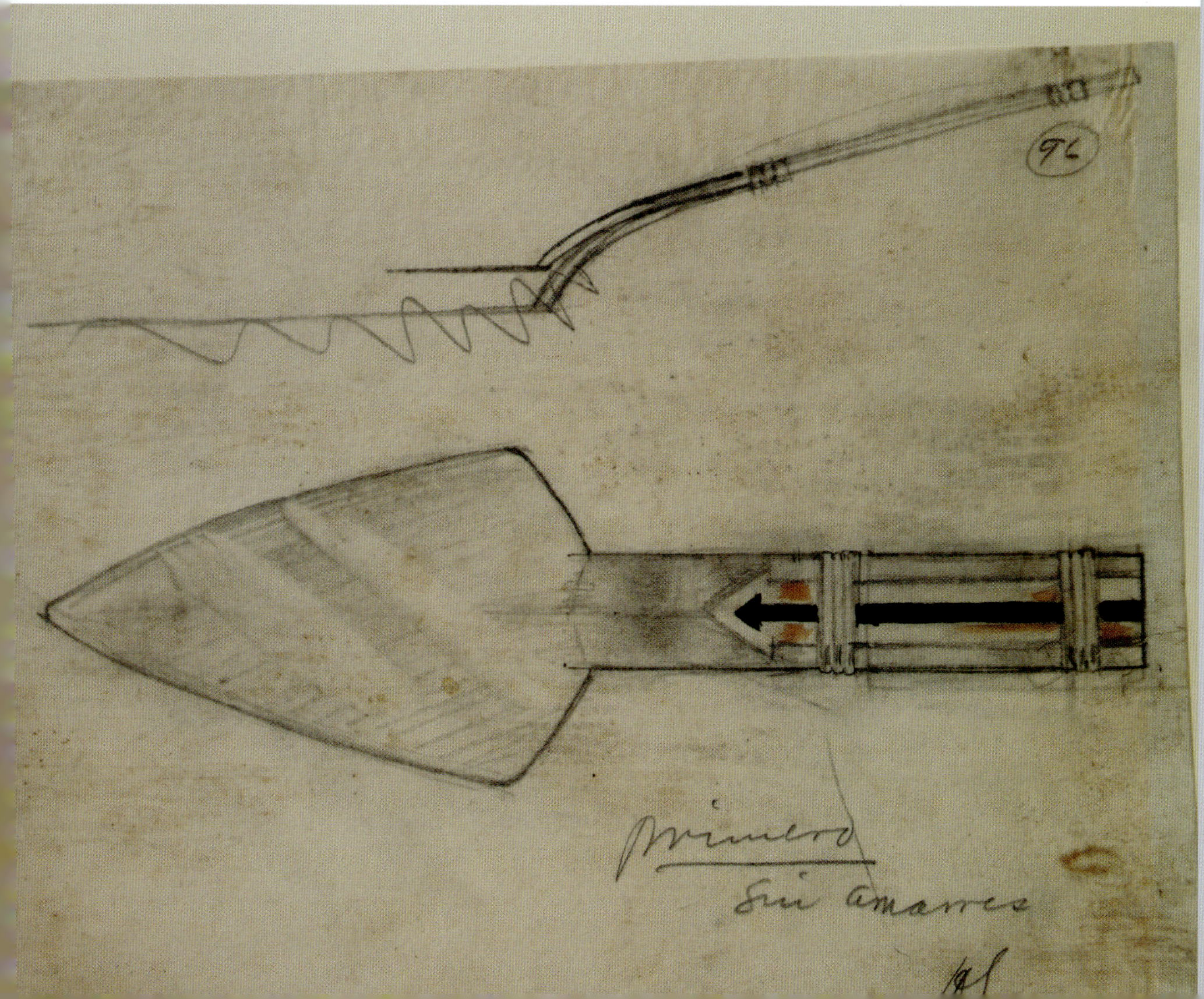

PS 176. Original design drawing. Courtesy of Sucesores de Wm Spratling, S.A. de C.V.

SS 177. Sugar spoon, Tlingit raven, abalone mounting, silver. Courtesy, National Museum of the American Indian, Smithsonian Institution

SS 177. Original design drawing. Courtesy of Sucesores de Wm Spratling, S.A. de C.V.

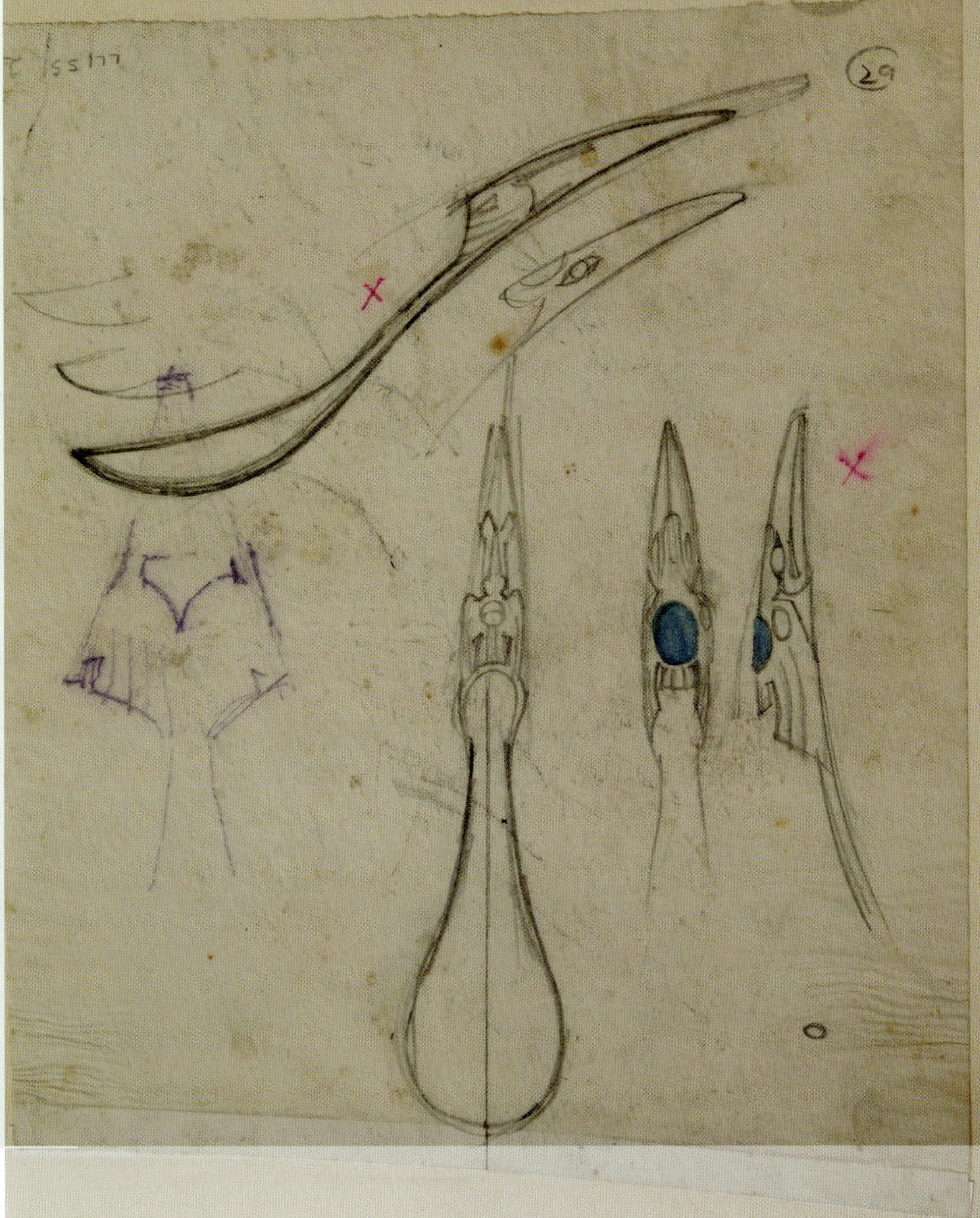

CHAPTER 5

Alberto Ulrich acquired Spratling's ranch at Taxco-el-Viejo in 1968, along with all of the remaining designs, molds and hallmarks that totaled 520 pieces. He already owned his friend William Spratling's former Taxco in-town house.

With the Spratling designs he acquired, Alberto Ulrich set up, in July of 1969, a new company, Sucesores de Wm Spratling, S. A. de C.V., to fabricate silver items and to continue producing and reissuing Spratling's original designs for jewelry and gift items.

Several of William Spratling's former workers stayed on at the ranch and produced silver designs on a small scale. One of those workers, Dom Tomas Vegas, had begun working for Spratling in 1938 at Las Delicias, when he was a young boy. He created items from Spratling's designs for almost sixty years and was the lone worker in the ranch workshop in 2009. Alberto Ulrich continued to run the new company until he, too, died, in November of 2002.

Today, Sucesores de William Spratling continues to operate under the guidance and management of Alberto Ulrich's two daughters, Violante Ulrich and Consuelo Ulrich. The company operated from the ranch outside Taxco until 2010, when the manufacturing operations were relocated to Mexico City. Even before then, the jewelry lines had been expanded to include items designed by both of the Ulrich sisters. The new designs are clearly reflections of William Spratling's work, by the designers Violante Ulrich, Consuelo Ulrich, and the team of Jason Creagh and Violante Ulrich. The clean lines demonstrate modern styles, while many of the designs reflect ancient Mexican forms from which they derive.

ALBERTO ULRICH & SUCESORES DE WM SPRATLIN

LEGACY

Alberto Ulrich. Courtesy of Sucesores de Wm Spratling, S.A. de C.V.

G, S. A. DE C.V.

Jason Creagh and Violante Ulrich. Buttons of wood and silver.

Violante Ulrich. Link bracelet and matching pin with wooden dots design, silver.

Violante Ulrich. Top bracelet, silver. Bottom bracelet, wooden dots, silver.

Alberto Ulrich in the on-site showroom at the ranch (formerly Spratling's museum).

TS-24. The silver mark of Sucesores de Wm Spratling, S.A. de C.V.

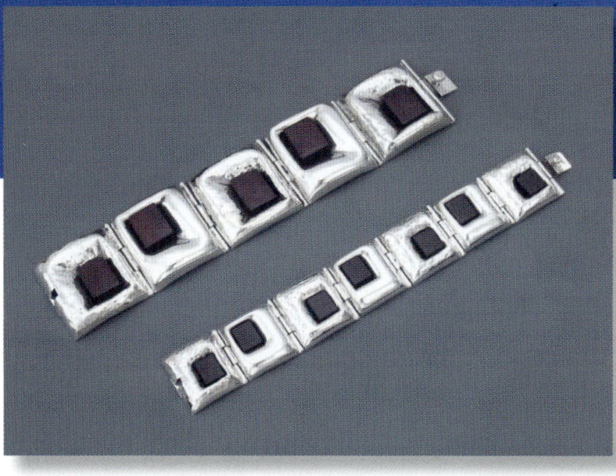

Violante Ulrich. Link bracelet, silver.

Violante Ulrich. Two bracelets with square links, each set with rosewood inlay, silver.

Violante Ulrich. Two link bracelets, silver.

Eagle pin. Sucesores de Wm Spratling, S.A. de C.V.

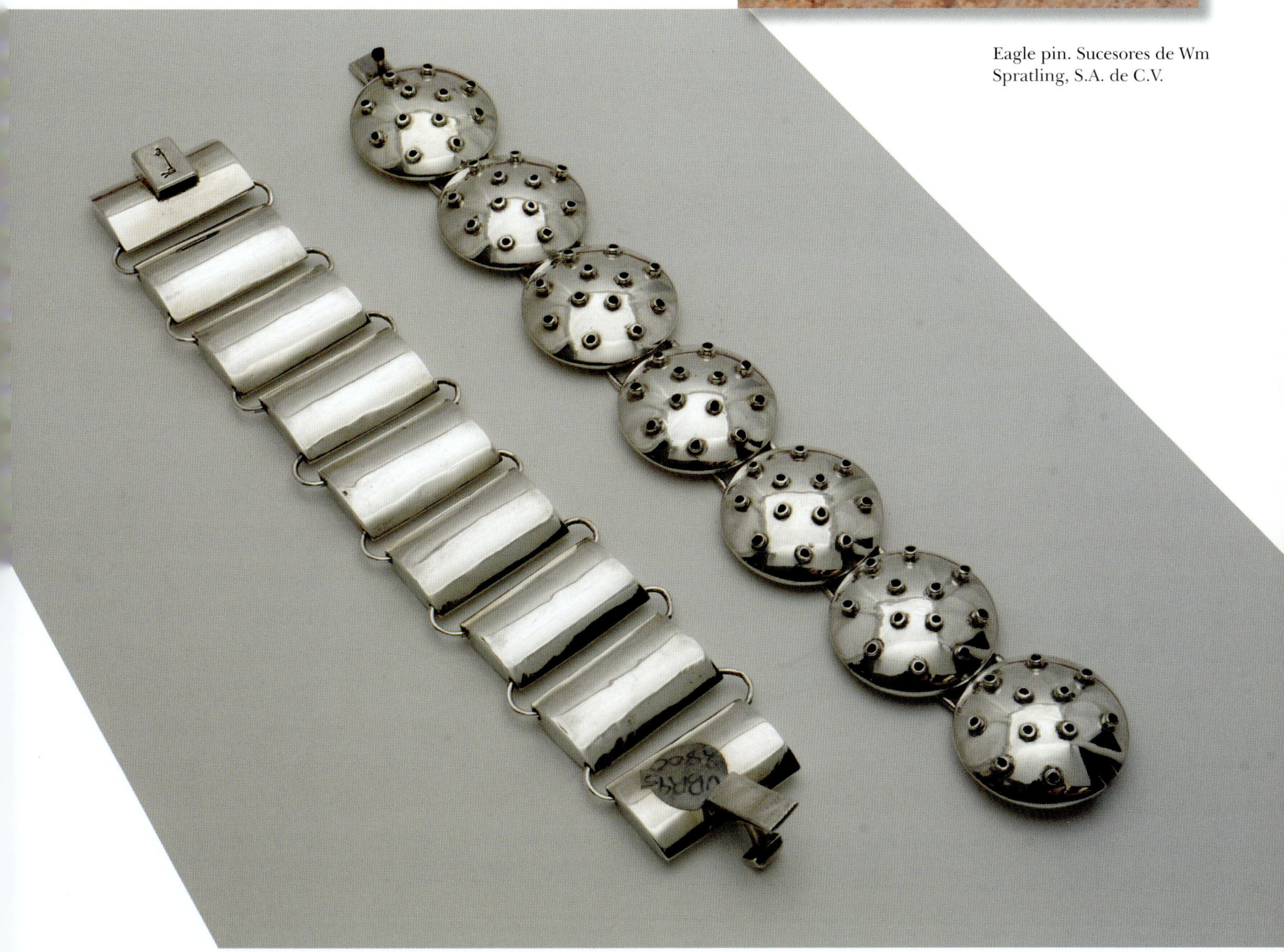

Jason Creagh and Violante Ulrich. Left bracelet, silver; right bracelet silver with wood inlay.

Violante Ulrich. Earrings, wood inlay and silver.

Jason Creagh and Violante Ulrich. Two bracelets, wood inlay and silver.

Jason Creagh and Violante Ulrich. Earrings and two bracelets, wood inlay and silver.

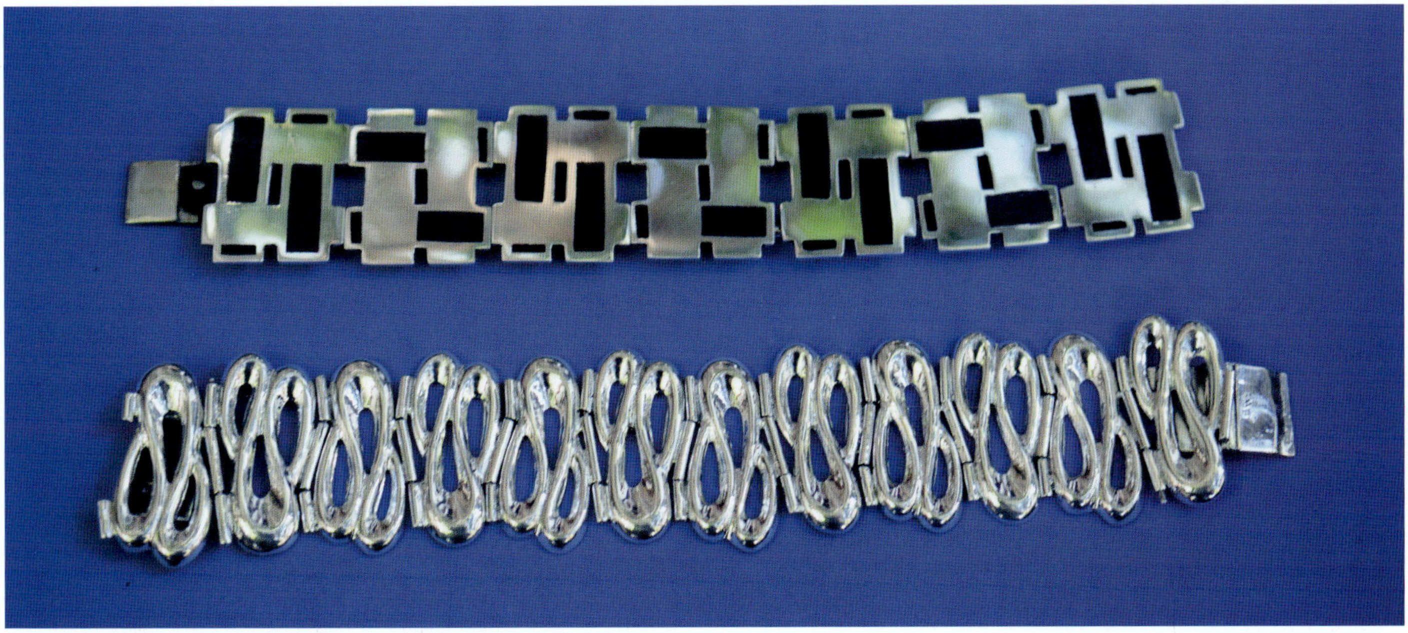

Jason Creagh and Violante Ulrich. Two bracelets, silver, one with wood inlay.

Violante Ulrich. Earrings of silver.

Violante Ulrich. Earrings of silver.

Violante Ulrich. Earrings of silver.

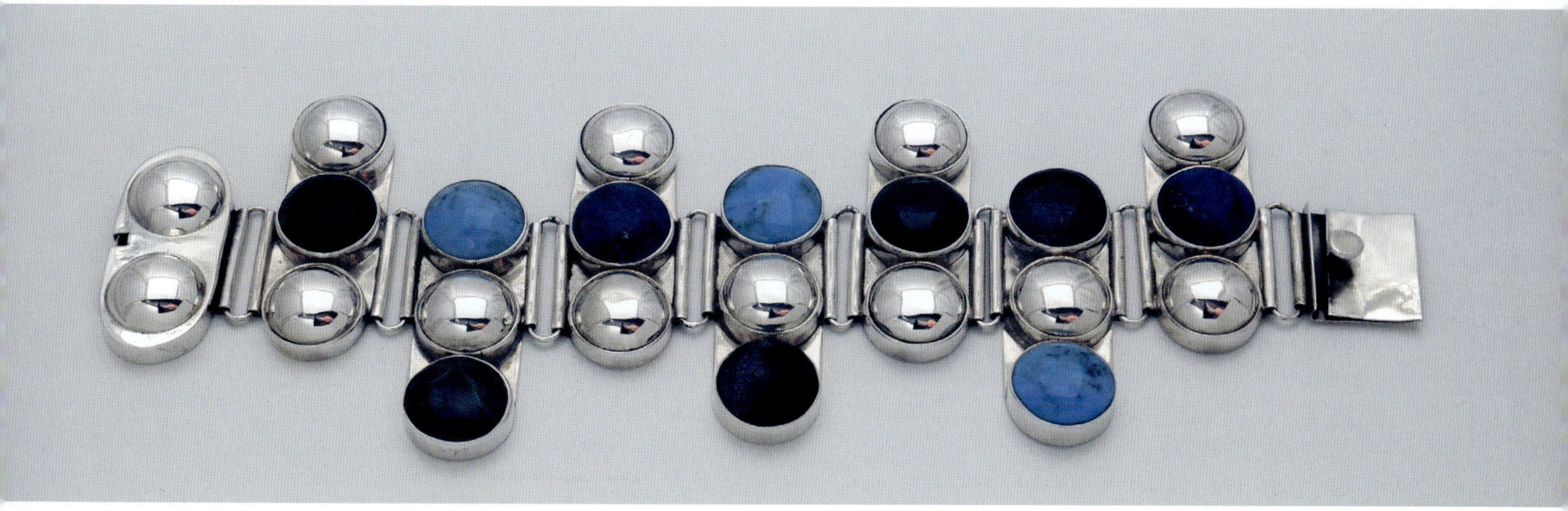

Violante Ulrich. Bracelet of jade, turquoise, amethyst, and silver links.

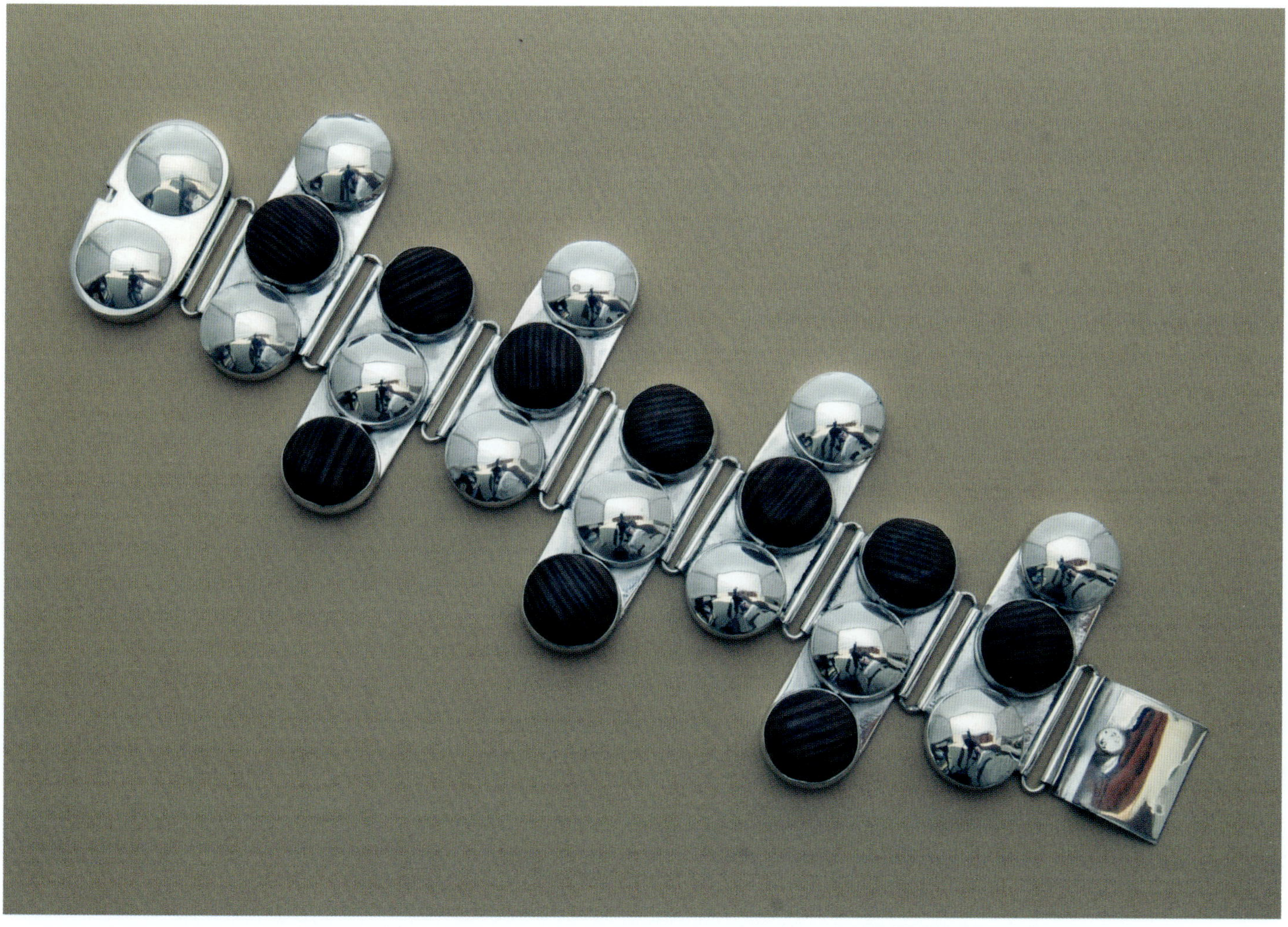

Violante Ulrich. Bracelet of wood and silver links.

Violante Ulrich. Necklace of wood inlay and silver.

Violante Ulrich. Necklace of wood inlay and silver.

Violante Ulrich. Necklace, wood and silver.

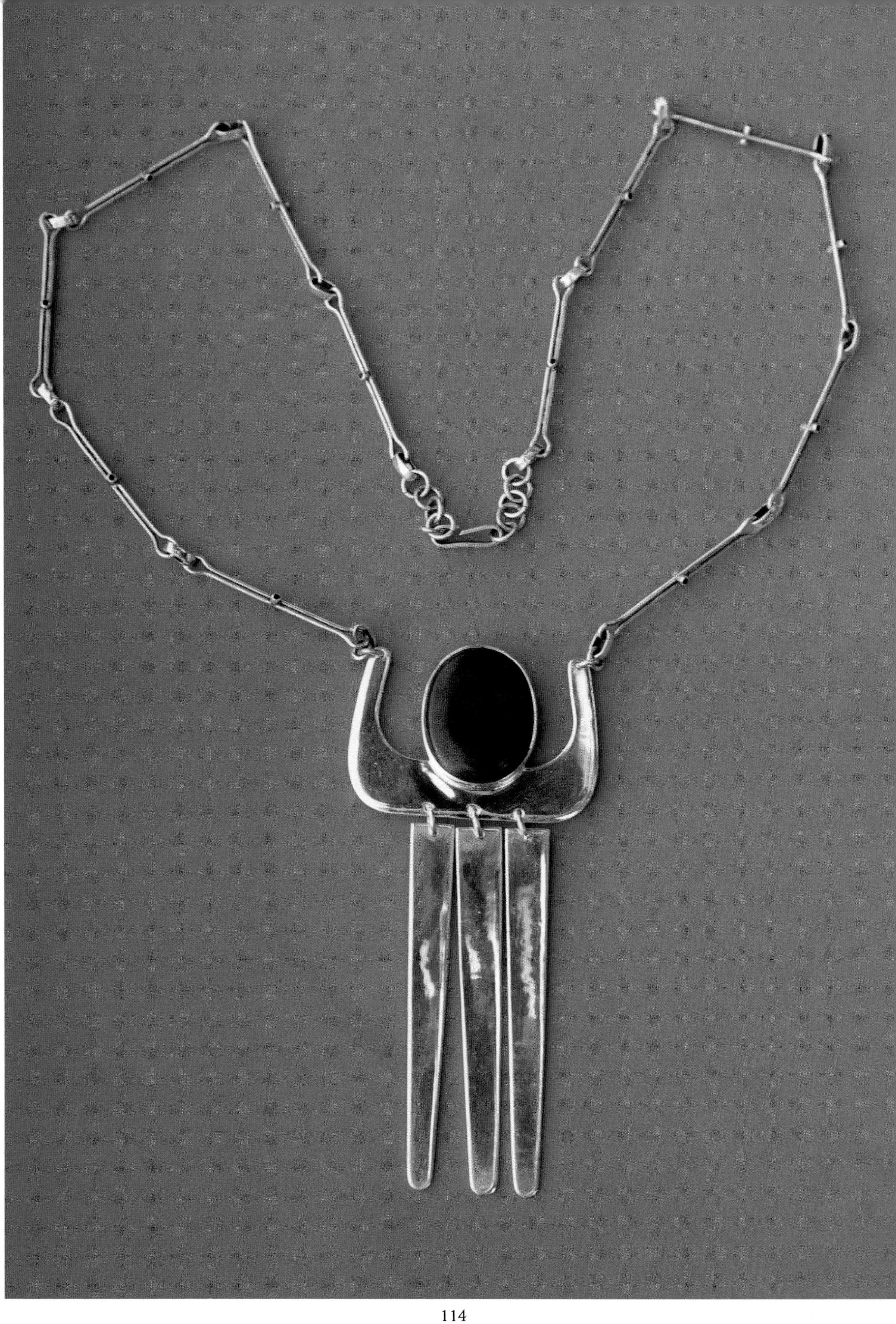

Violante Ulrich. Two necklaces, wood and silver.

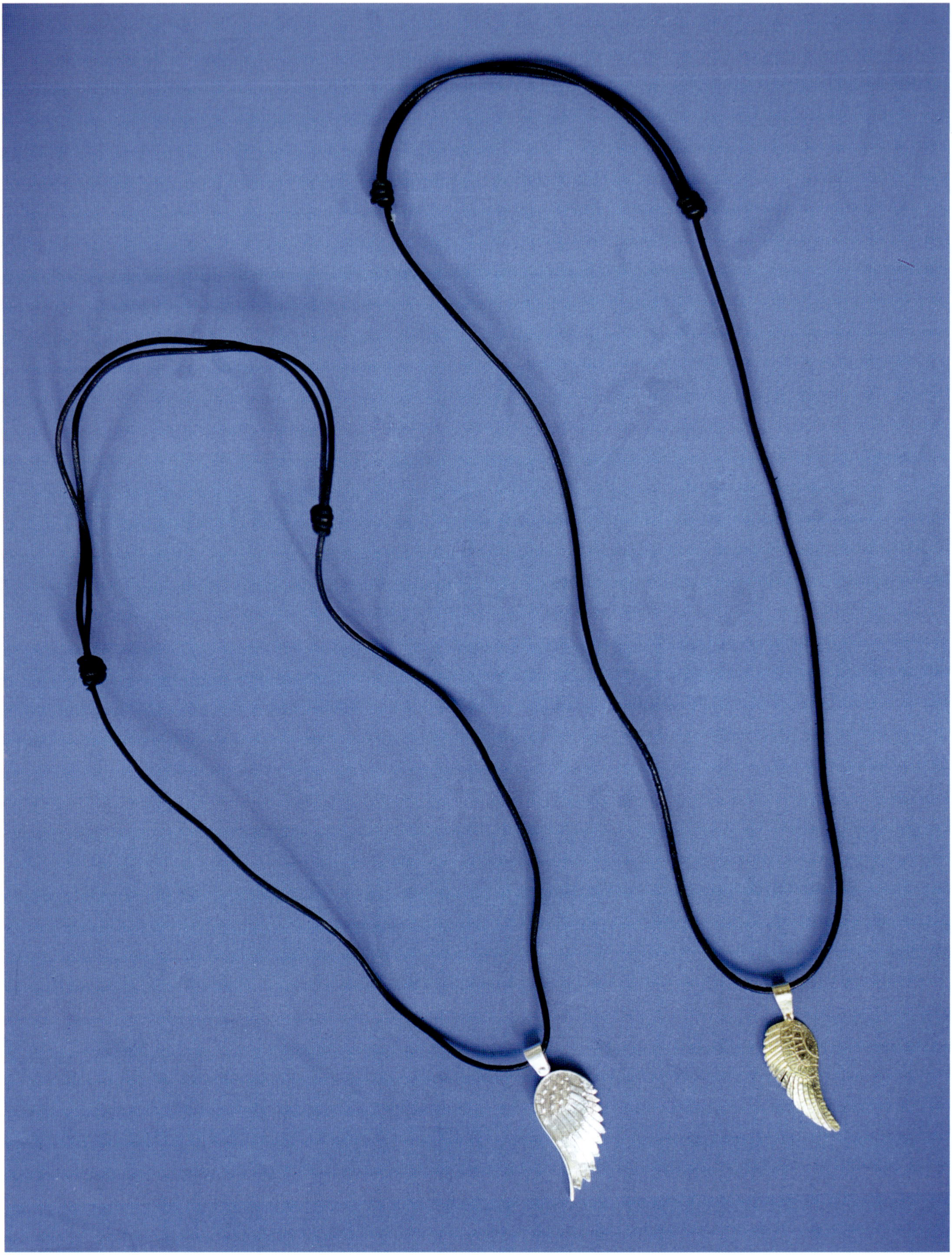

Violante Ulrich. Necklace, wood and silver.

Violante Ulrich. Two necklaces, Leather cord and gold feather pendants.

Violante Ulrich. Necklace, tortoise shell and silver links.

Violante Ulrich. Necklace of amethyst and silver beads.

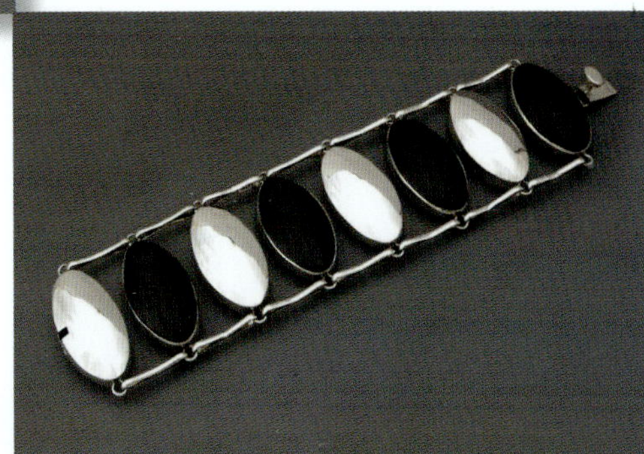

Violante Ulrich. Link bracelet with matte onyx and silver.

Violante Ulrich. Three rings of silver.

Jason Creagh and Violante Ulrich.
Necklace and bracelet, wood and silver.

Violante Ulrich. Necklace, wood and silver.

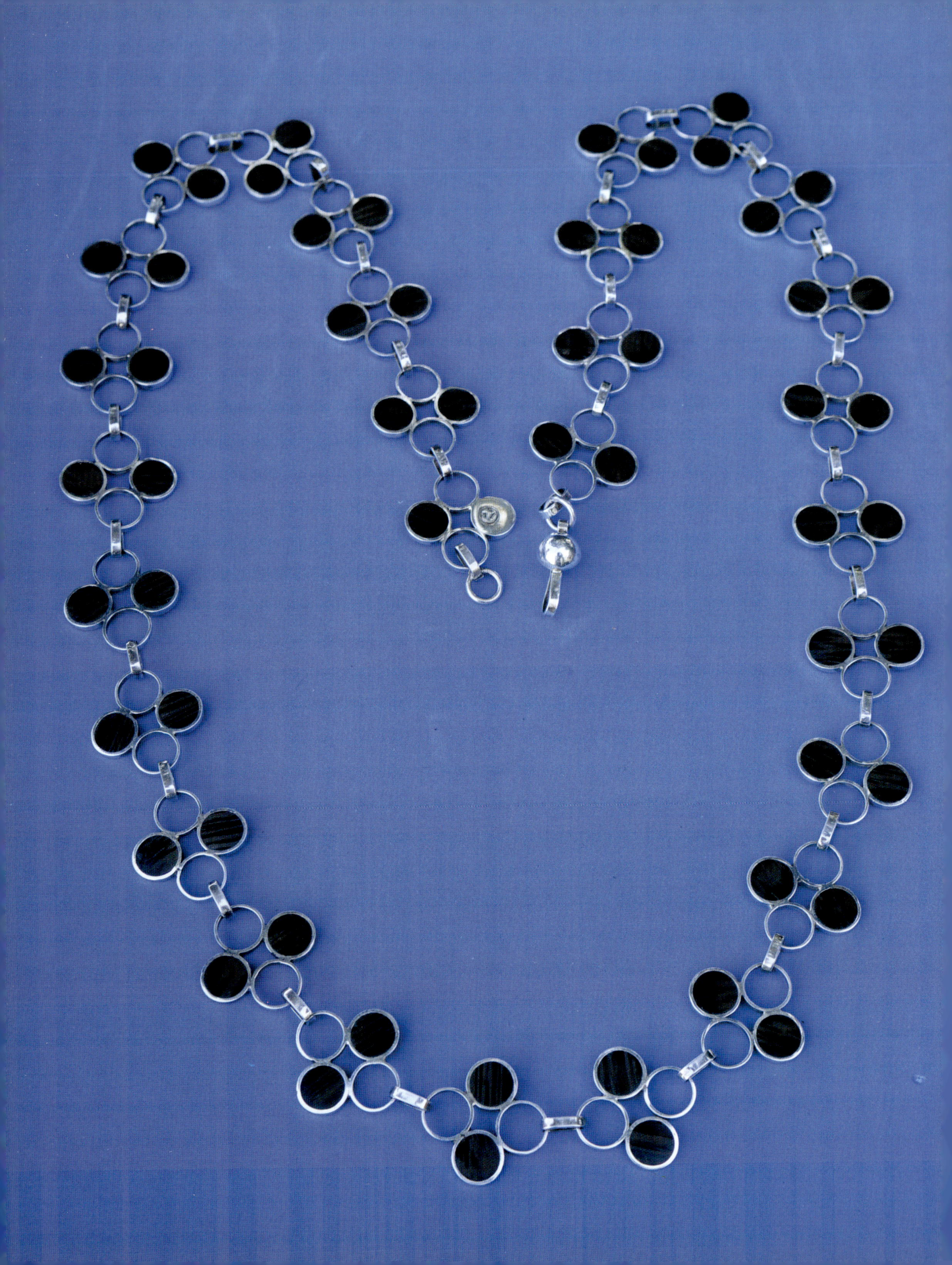

Jason Creagh and Violante Ulrich. Necklace, wood inlay and silver.

Jason Creagh and Violante Ulrich. Cuff bracelet with wooden squares inlaid in silver.

Jason Creagh and Violante Ulrich. Bracelet with wood inlay and silver.

Jason Creagh and Violante Ulrich. Necklace, coral and silver.

Violante Ulrich. Necklace with wood inlay and silver wire.

Violante Ulrich. Necklace with small wooden inlay and silver wire.

Violante Ulrich. Two bracelets with fossil bone and silver chain.

Jason Creagh and Violante Ulrich. Two necklaces, wood and silver.

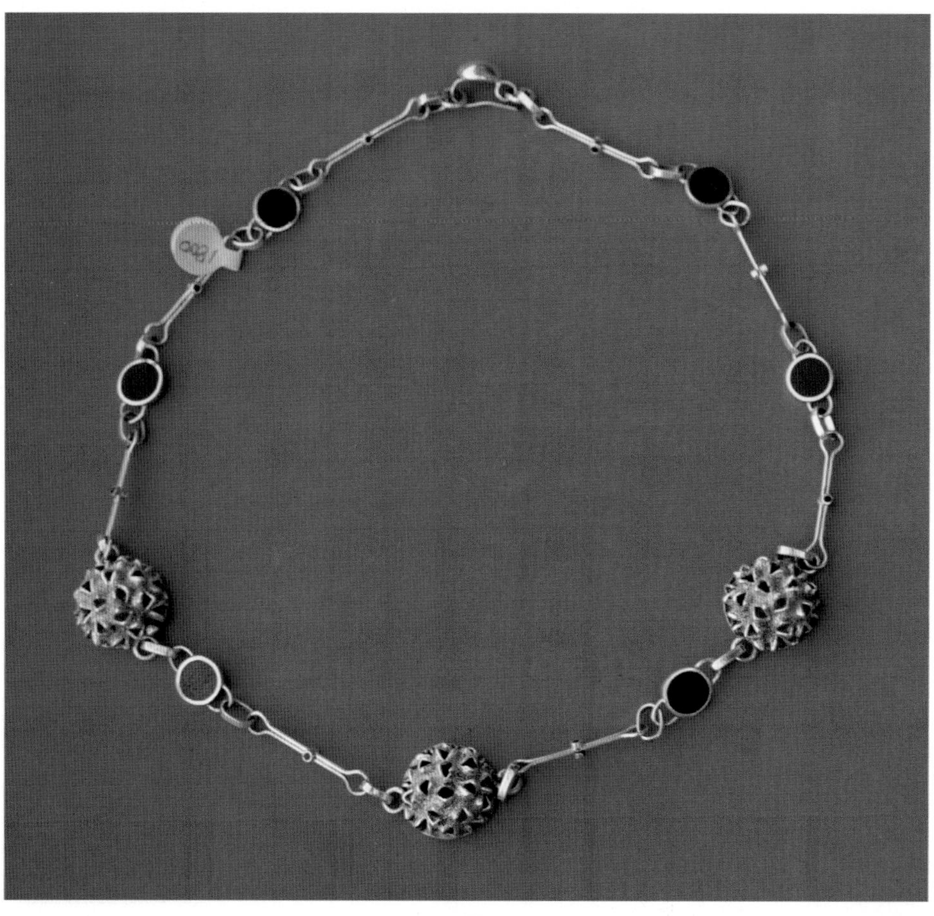

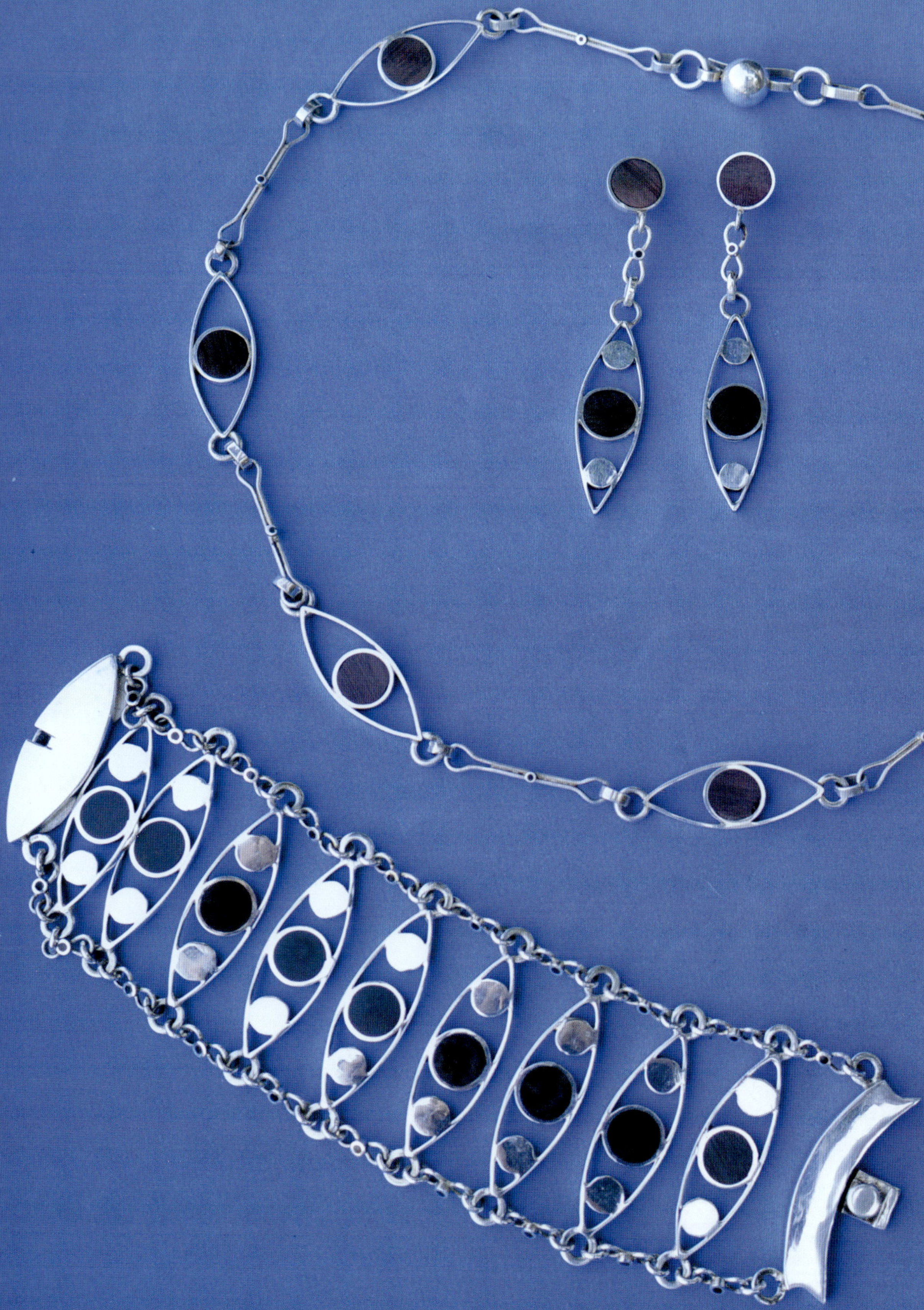

Jason Creagh and Violante Ulrich. Necklace with matching bracelet and earrings, wood and silver wire.

Violante Ulrich. Cuff bracelet with amethyst dots and silver.

Jason Creagh and Violante Ulrich. Belt of silver wire links

Violante Ulrich. Cuff bracelet of silver with three fossil ivories.

Violante Ulrich. Cuff bracelet with nine amethyst beads and silver.

Violante Ulrich. Cuff bracelet of silver with four amethysts.

Consuelo Ulrich. Necklace with silver link chain and carved jade and 18K gold design of leaf fronds.

Consuelo Ulrich. Necklace of leather cord and a large stone, with 18K gold button inset.

Consuelo Ulrich. Necklace of braided leather cord and jade disc in 18K gold supports.

Consuelo Ulrich. Bracelet, on braided leather, jade carving and 18K gold supports.

Consuelo Ulrich. Necklace of 18K gold, with beads of jade and ivory and a gold hand design.

Consuelo Ulrich. Earrings of 18K gold in a hand design.

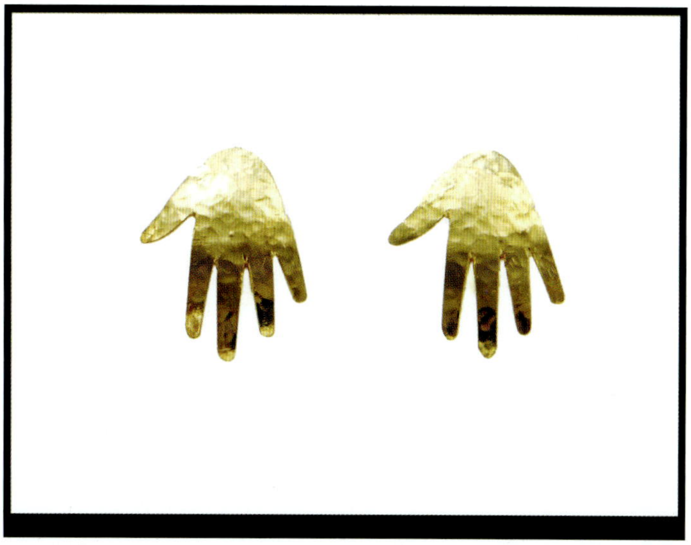

Consuelo Ulrich. Necklace of braided leather and five carved jade and 18K gold beads.

Consuelo Ulrich. Earrings in the form of butterflies with diamonds, sapphires, and 18K gold

Consuelo Ulrich. Bracelet on braided leather, jade carving and 18K gold supports.

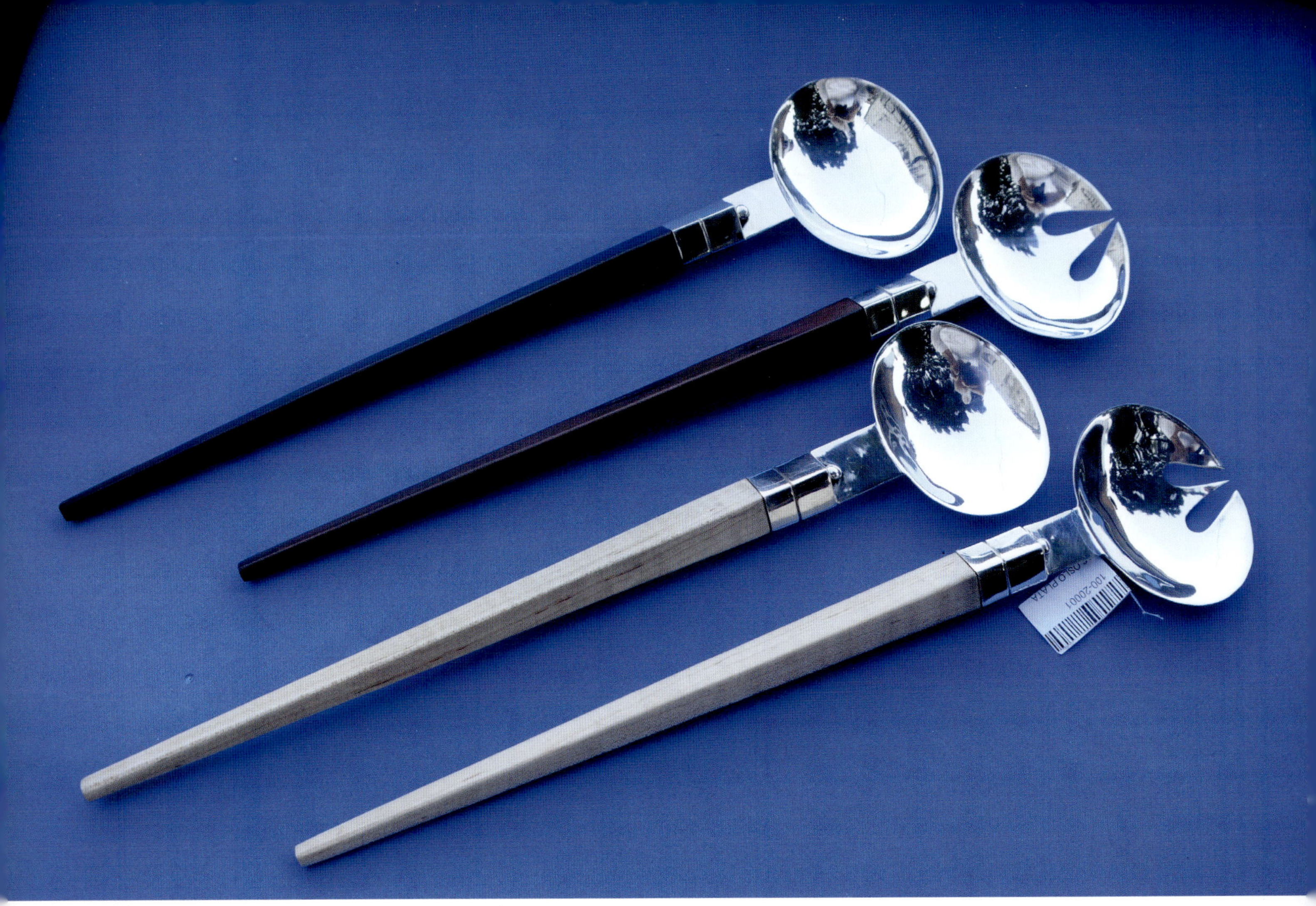

Jason Creagh and Violante Ulrich. Four soup spoons, wood and silver

Jason Creagh and Violante Ulrich. 6-piece flatware place setting, wood design and silver.

Jason Creagh and Violante Ulrich. Six soup spoons, wood and silver.

Jason Creagh and Violante Ulrich. 6-piece flatware place service, wood and silver.

William Spratling design. Wine glass, redesigned by Alberto Ulrich using glass in place of silver, c. 1980.

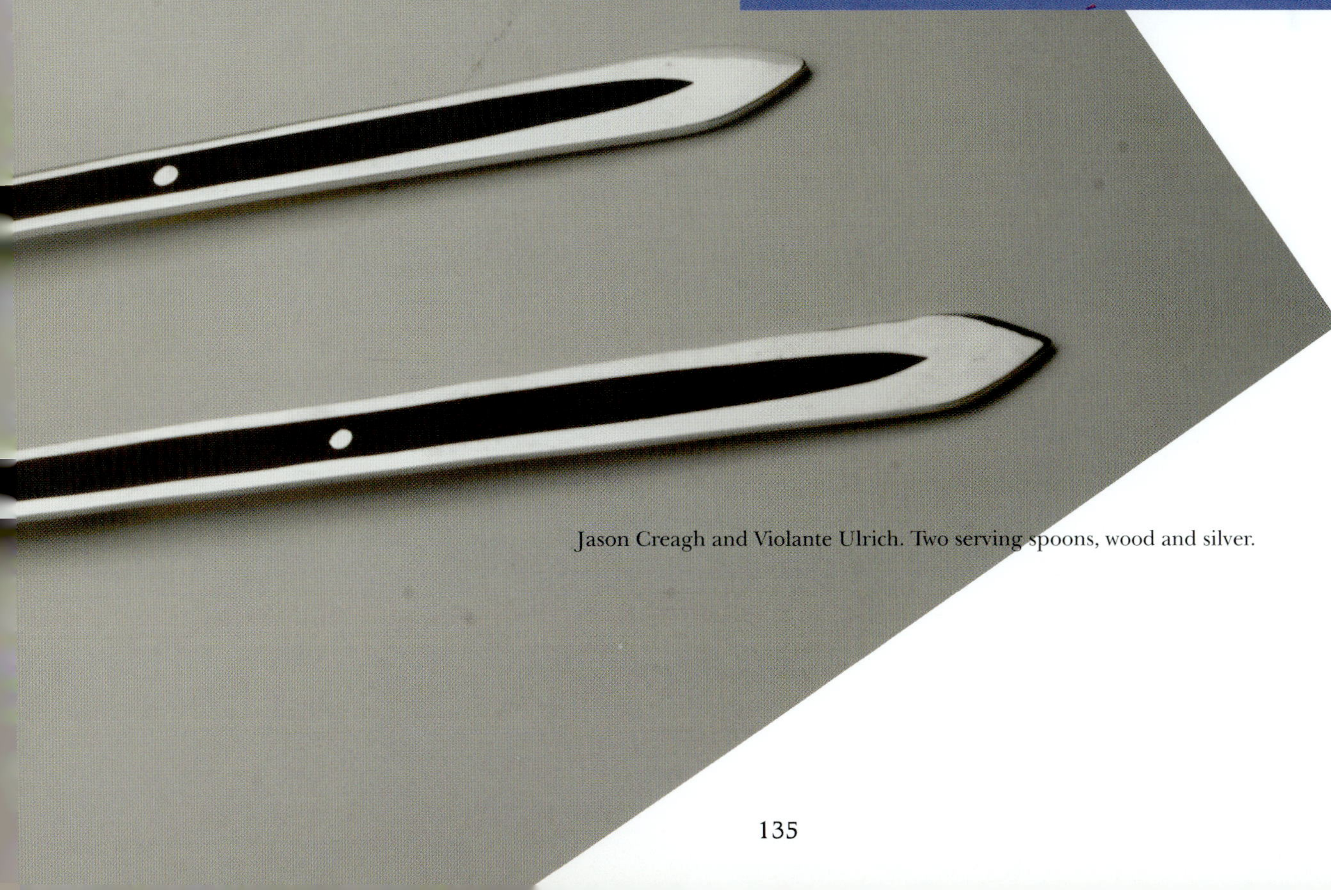

Jason Creagh and Violante Ulrich. Two serving spoons, wood and silver.

Jason Creagh and Violante Ulrich. 5-piece flatware place service, wood and silver.

Jason Creagh and Violante Ulrich. Six spoons, wood and silver.

Jason Creagh and Violante Ulrich. Six spoons, wood and silver.

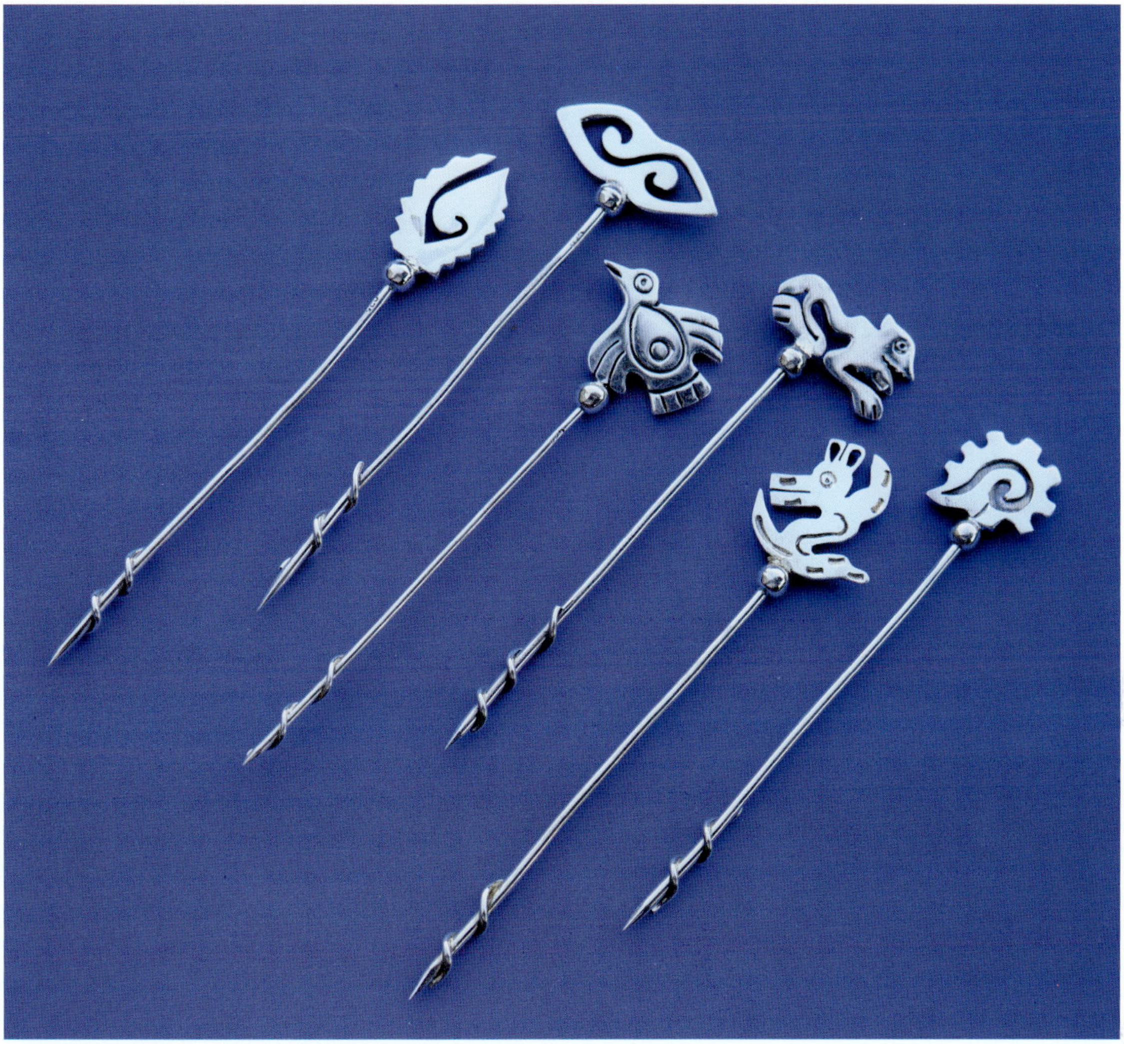

Jason Creagh and Violante Ulrich. Six martini picks, silver.

Jason Creagh and Violante Ulrich. Six martini picks, wood and silver.

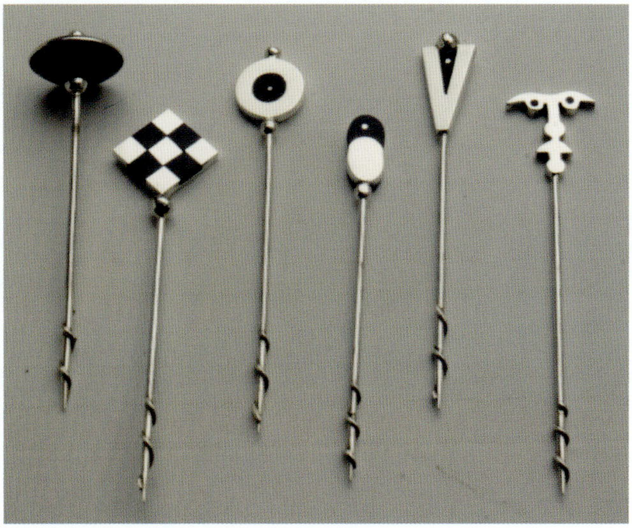

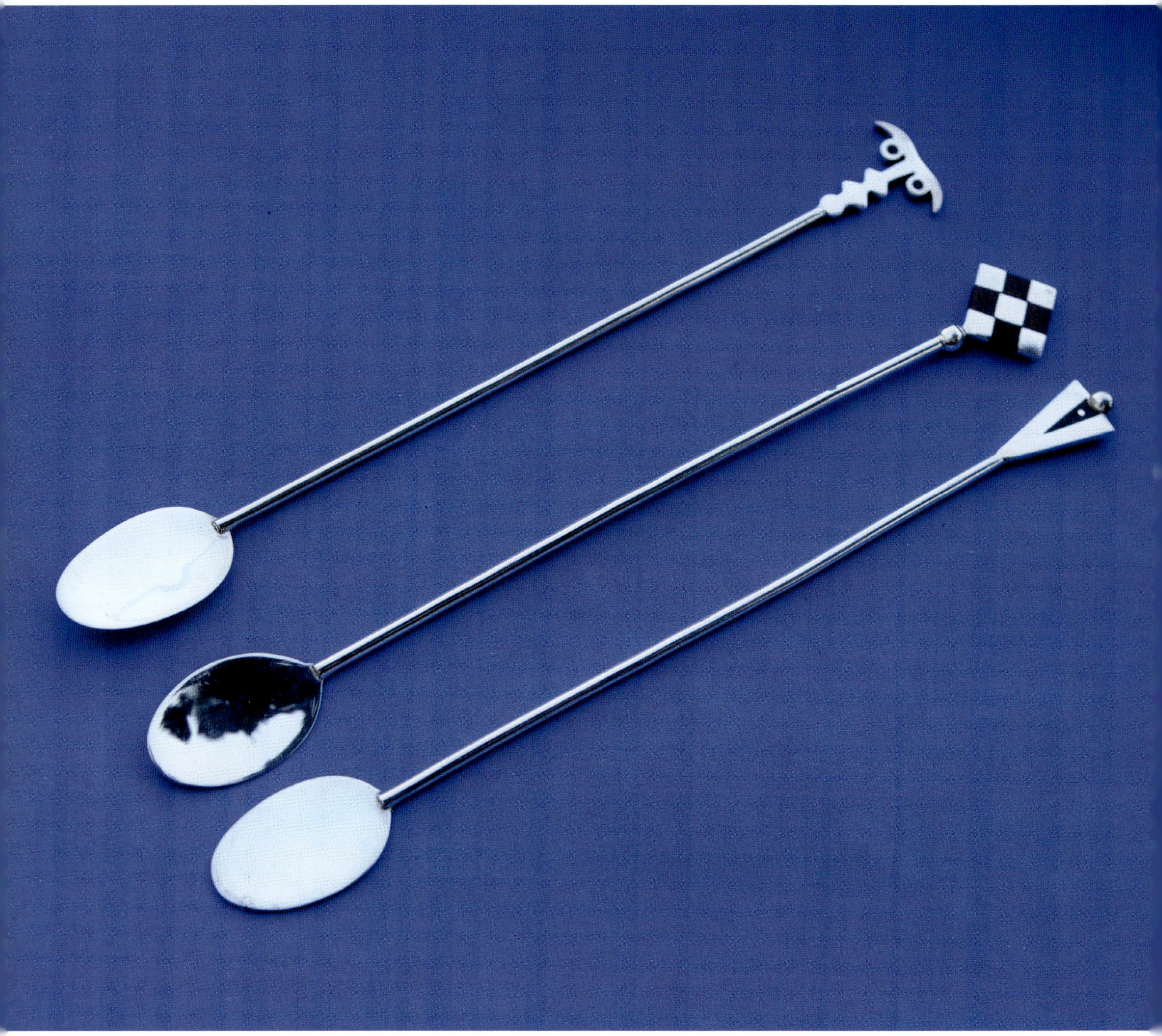

Jason Creagh and Violante Ulrich. Three swizzle sticks, wood and silver.

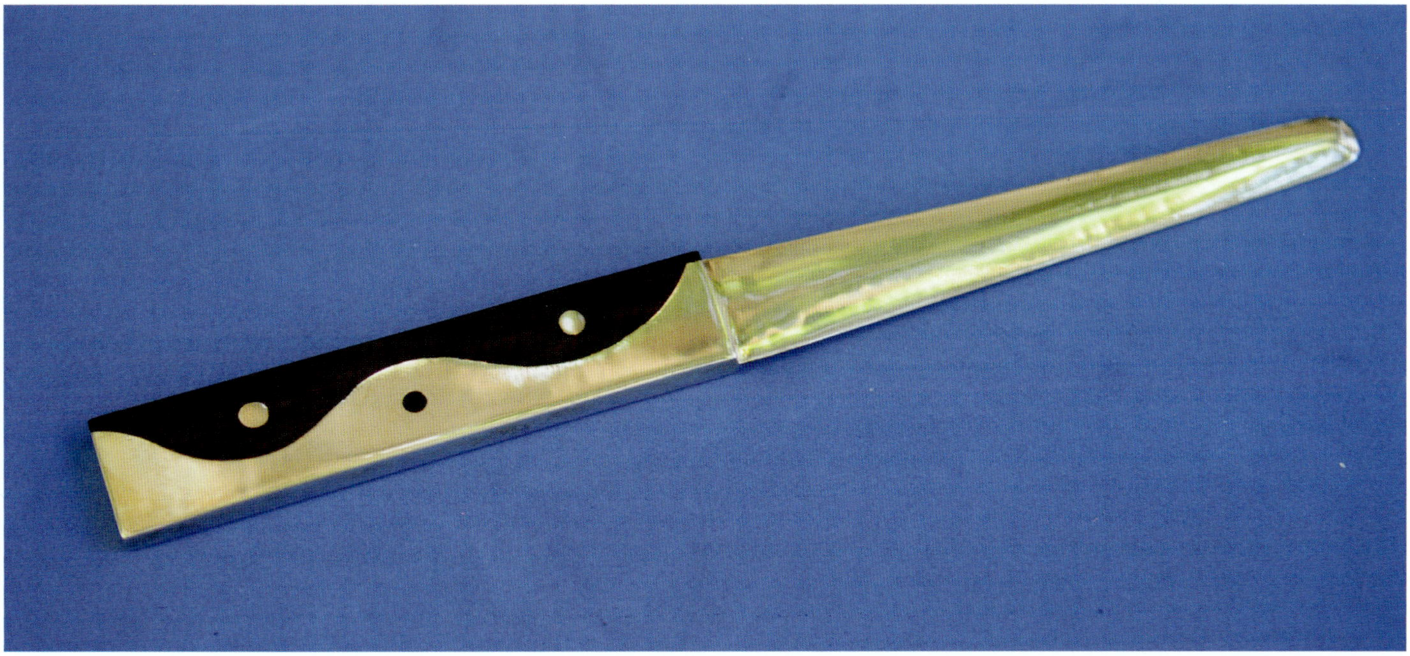

Jason Creagh and Violante Ulrich. Letter opener, wood and silver.

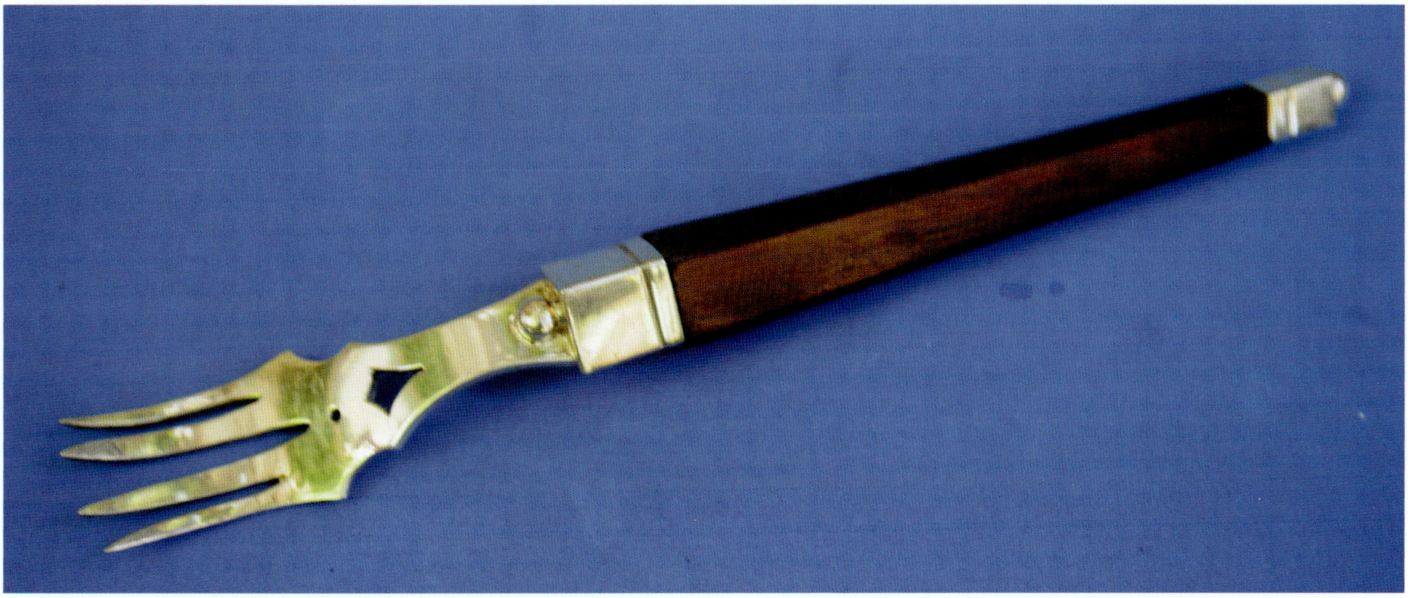

Violante Ulrich. Serving fork, wood and silver.

Violante Ulrich. Salt and pepper shakers, silver on a wooden base.

Jason Creagh and Violante Ulrich. Pie-serving spatula, wood and silver.

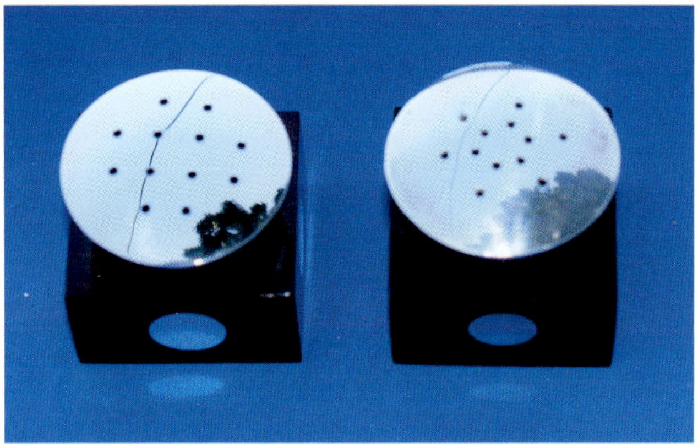

Jason Creagh and Violante Ulrich. Short salt and pepper shakers of wood and silver.

Pitcher. silver. Sucesores de Wm Spratling, S.A. de C.V.

Jason Creagh and Violante Ulrich. Tall salt and pepper shakers of wood and silver.

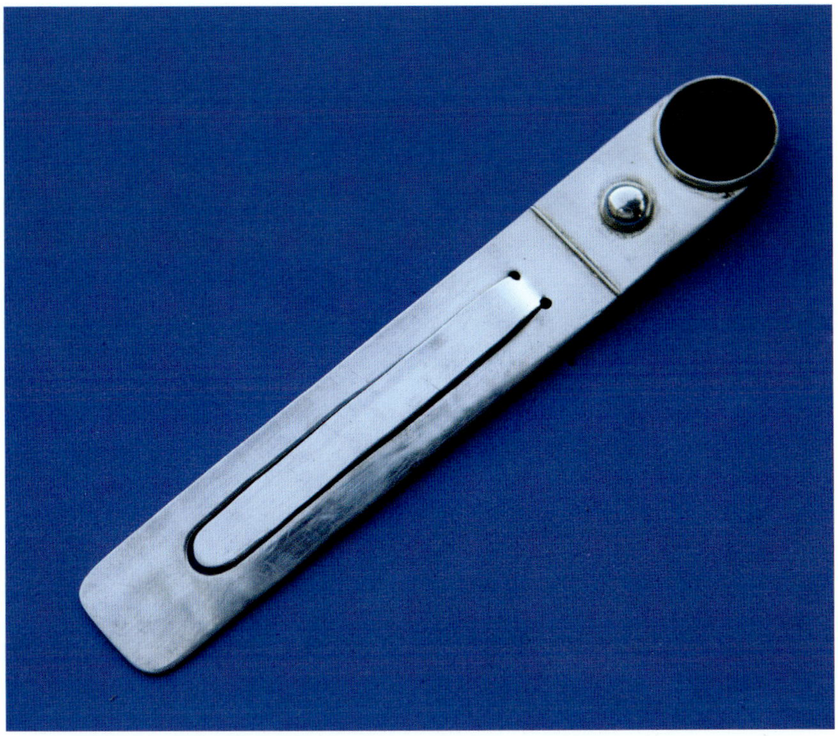

Violante Ulrich. Bookmark, wood and silver

Violante Ulrich. Buttons of wood inlay and silver.

Violante Ulrich. Two hair combs of silver.

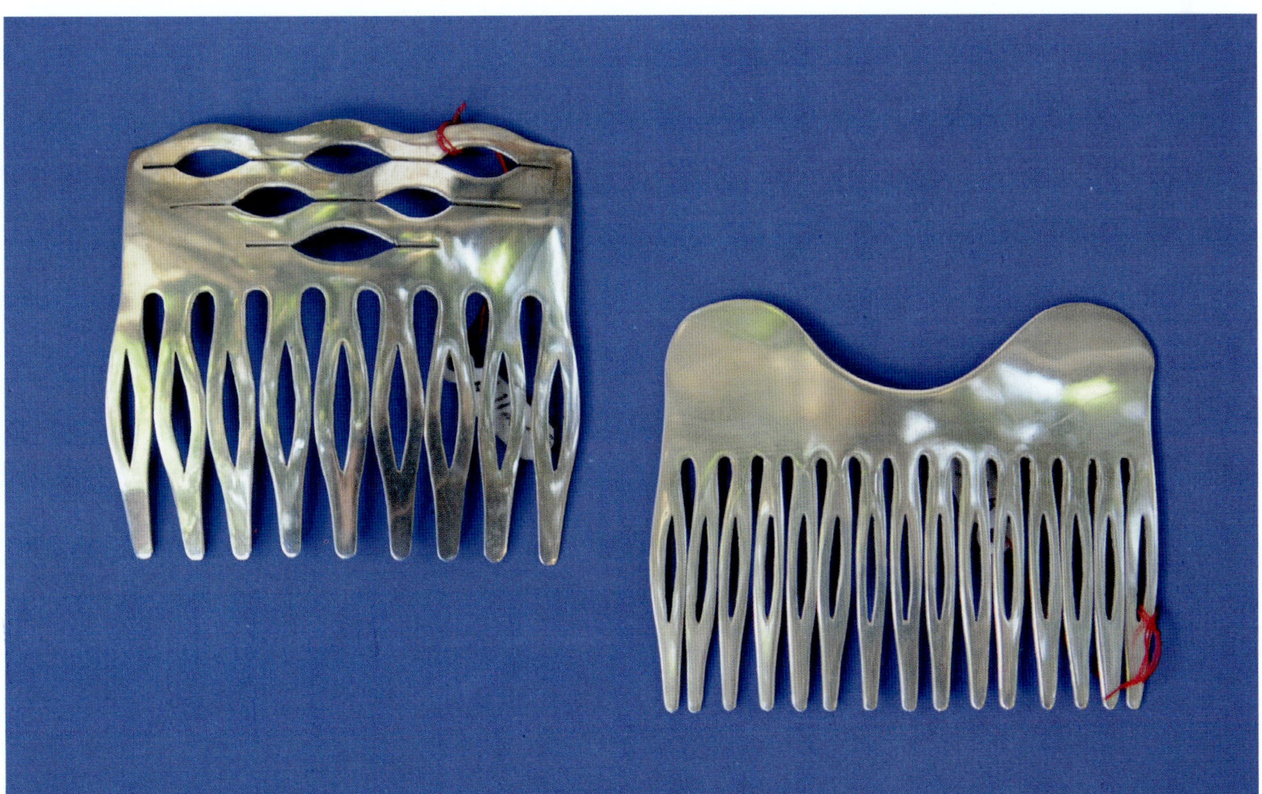

Violante Ulrich. Silver dice.

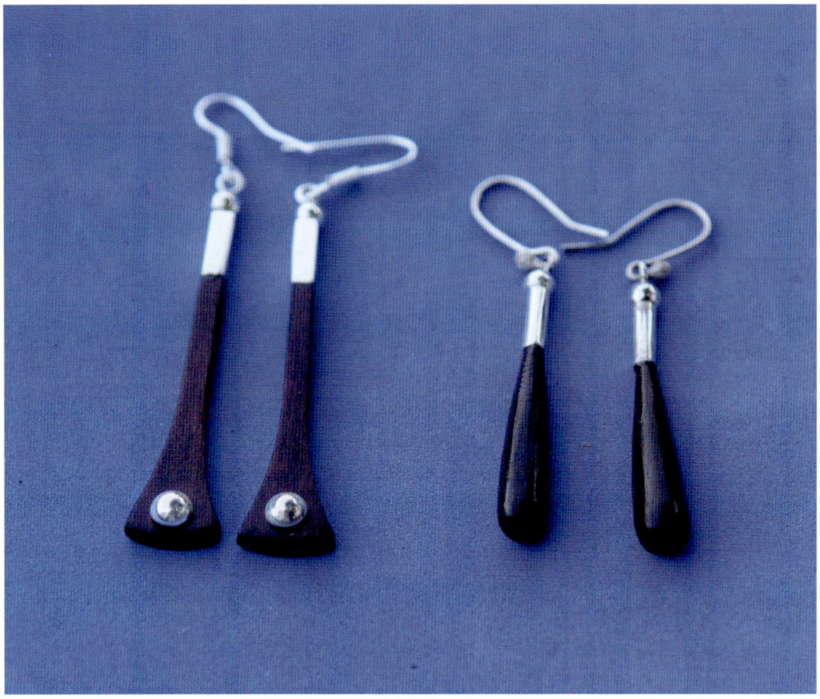

Violante Ulrich. Two pair of earrings, wood and silver.

Jason Creagh and Violante Ulrich. Pen box of wood with silver inlay.

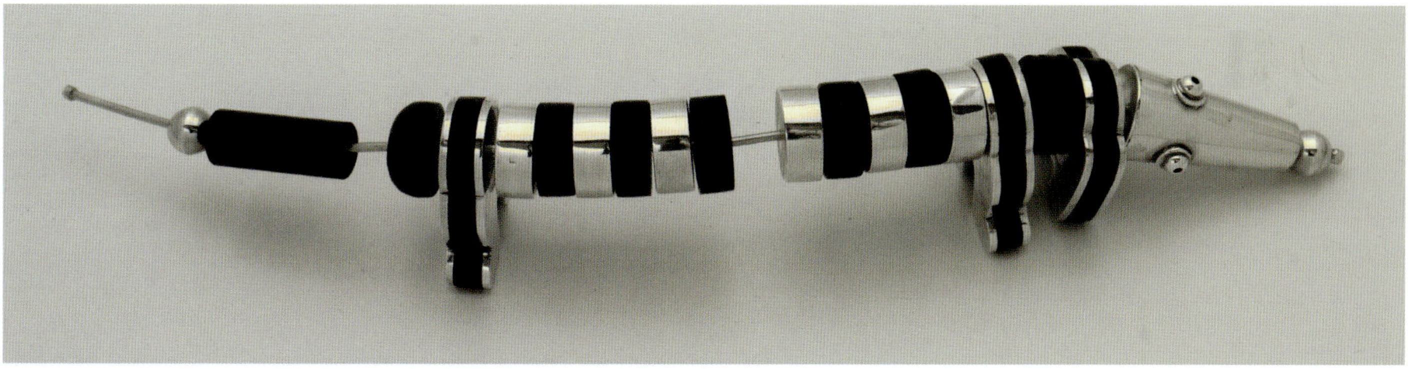

Violante Ulrich. Basset hound figure of wood and silver.

Violante Ulrich. Candle holder of silver on a wooden base.

Violante Ulrich. Candlestick of wood and silver rings.

Violante Ulrich. Flower holder, silver on a wooden base.

William Spratling

1900
William Spratling born September 22 in Sonyea, Livingston County, New York

1910
Attended Calvert School in Baltimore, Maryland

1911–1912
Living in Summit, New Jersey. Mother and sister Wilhelmina died

1912–1914 Living in Atlanta, Georgia, with an uncle; Father died

1915
Attended Auburn High School in Auburn, Alabama

1918
Graduated from high school and entered Auburn Polytechnic Institute, where he majored in architecture

1919–1921
Instructor in the architecture department at Auburn Polytechnic Institute

In the summers was a draftsman for T. C. I. in Birmingham, Alabama

1900 1910 1920

TIMELINE

1926
Wrote a book with neighbor William Faulkner, *Sherwood Anderson and Other Famous Creoles*

1927
Wrote "Some Impressions of Mexico," for *Architectural Forum*

Wrote a book with Natalie Scott, *Old Plantation Houses in Louisiana*

1928
Wrote "Cane River Portraits" for *Scribner's Magazine*

Assisted Fred Davis in renovations to a house, Casa Mañana, in Cuernavaca

1926–1929
Summer School lectures given on architecture in Mexico at the National University of Mexico

1922–1929
Associate Professor of Architecture at Tulane, University in New Orleans, Louisiana

1923
Published *The Art of Pencil Drawing* and illustrated *Picturesque New Orleans*.

Summer travel to France

1924
Summer travel to Italy

1925
Wrote article "Architectural Traditions in New Orleans" with Nathaniel Courtland Curtis for *The Journal of the American Institute of Architects*

1929
Spratling's friend, muralist Diego Rivera, received a gold medal from American Institute of Architects Fine Arts Committee

Purchased a house, Casa Delicias, in Taxco

Writing the book *Little Mexico*

Wrote "Figures in a Mexican Renaissance," for *Scribner's Magazine*

Wrote "Indo-Hispanic Mexico, I and II," for *Architecture*

Helped organize, with George Biddle and Carl Zigrosser, an exhibit of French and American art at Escuela de Bellas Artes in Mexico City

Sent a tracing of the 16th century linen map of Mexico, *Lienzo de Noxtepec*, that included a history of the Rio Balsas region in Guerrero, to Tulane University

WILLIAM SPRATLING

1930
Wrote "Diego Rivera" in *Mexican Folkways*

Helped organize exhibit of Mexican art for the Metropolitan Museum of Art, New York

1931
Illustrated book by Natalie Scott, *Two Hundred Years of New Orleans Cooking*

Wrote "Some New Discoveries in Mexican Clay" for *International Studio*

Illustrated book by Manuel Toussanint, *Tasco.*

Lithograph "Niño" exhibited at Weyhe Gallery

Established his silver workshop, Taller de Las Delicias, at his home, Casa Delicias, in Taxco,

Prepared catalog for Diego Rivera's exhibition at the Museum of Modern Art in New York

Published *Siqueiros: 13 Woodcuts*

1932
Published *Little Mexico*

Illustrated Elizabeth Morrow's book *Casa Mañana*

Work in the Weyhe Gallery exhibit, *Mexican Graphic Art*

1933
Moved his workshop, Taller de Las Delicias, to Casa Verdugo de Aragones

Designed and built Hotel Rancho Telva

1937
Wrote "Modern Mexican Silversmithing" for *Mexican Art and Life*

1930 1940

1940–1941
Registered the Silson patents in the United States

1941
Silson, Inc. of New York produced items from Spratling's designs

TIMELINE

1943–1946
Montgomery Ward catalogs feature Spratling silver

1944
Published illustrated catalog of his silver items, *Fine Mexican Silver*

Sold shares in his company, Spratling y Artesanos, as Managing Director and formed a Board of Directors

Completed renovation of La Florida

Article on the workshop in *Nosotros*

1945
Resigned as Managing Director of Spratling y Artesanos and contracted with the company to supply designs for silver items

Moved his residence to the ranch at Taxco-el-Viejo

Traveled to Alaska in August and September

Spratling y Artesanos registered hallmarks "WS" and "Spratling"

Completed the Report on Alaska arts and Crafts in October

1946
Sold his shares in Spratling y Artesanos

Movie *The Man From New Orleans* about William Spratling released

1947
Movie *The Fugative* filmed at Spratling's ranch

1948
Flew to Alaska and traveled there September to November

1949
Contracted with Conquistador to provide designs and models
Seven Alaska natives trained at the Spratling ranch, January to March

200 Alaskan models completed in April and sent to Washington, D.C.

Congress does not appropriate funds for Alaska project

New models made for Conquistador line "Spratling Silver in Mexico"

1949 – 1952
Attempts made to revive the Alaska project

William Spratling

1950
Registered the script "WS" hallmark in Mexico

Cancelled the Conquistador contract

Formed the company William Spratling, S. A.

1949 – 1952
Attempts made to revive the Alaska project

1951
Registered the script "WS" hallmark in the United States

1953
Named "Hijo Predilecto" of Taxco and a street named for him, Calle de Guillermo Spratling

First National Silver Fair held in June

1955
Wrote "25 Years of Mexican Silverware" for *Arte de México*

1956
Wrote "The True Color of Silver is White" for *Mexico This Month*

1959
Donated Remojades ceramic sculpture to National Autonomous University of Mexico

1960
Wrote *More Human Than Devine*, published in English and Spanish by National Autonomous University of Mexico

1950

1960

TIMELINE

1962
Received Doctor Honoris Causa degree from Auburn University

1963
Movie *Plateros y Tejedores de Taxco* filmed at Spratling's ranch

Donated items from his pre-Columbian collection to the National Museum of Anthropology in Mexico City

1964
Wrote exhibit catalog *Ancient Sculpture from Guerrero* for Museum of National Autonomous University of Mexico

Republished *Little Mexico* as a new title, *A Small Mexican World*

Crashed and lost his airplane, *"El Niño"*

1965
Translation of *A Small Mexican World* published as *México Tras Lomita*

Exhibit "Un Homenaje a William Spratling" at Instituto Mexicano, Norteamericano de Relaciones Culturales

Exhibit *The World of William Spratling* at McNay Art Institute, San Antonio, Texas, and at Otis Art Institute, Los Angeles, California

1966
Book *Sherwood Anderson and Other Famous Creoles* republished by University of Texas Press

Art collection excerpts exhibited at School of Design and Handicrafts at the National Institute of Fine Arts in Mexico City

1967
Approved final documents to establish the Museo de Taxco

Died after an automobile accident August 7

Posthumous publication of *File on Spratling*

Appendix

Alaska Report to the Indian Arts & Crafts Board of the U. S. Department of the Interior

R E P O R T :

A PLAN FOR ORGANIZING THE CRAFTS AND SMALLER INDUSTRIES (ALL MANUAL OR SEMI-MANUAL PRODUCTION) AND A POLICY FOR THEIR CONSTANT FUTURE DEVELOPMENT IN -

A L A S K A .

O C T O B E R , 1 9 4 5 .

WILLIAM SPRATLING

TAXCO EL VIEJO, GRO.,
MEXICO.

To the Chairman and Members of the Indian Arts and Crafts Board, United States Department of the Interior.

REPORT: A PLAN FOR ORGANIZING THE CRAFTS AND SMALLER INDUSTRIES (ALL MANUAL OR SEMI-MANUAL PRODUCTION AND A POLICY FOR THEIR CONSTANT FUTURE DEVELOPMENT IN ALASKA.

OBJECTIVE: to encourage, dignify and build up production of crafts which by tradition or association of materials and means belong to Alaska and have a right to be done there and not abroad.

Also, making use of existing channels for initial financing and marketing, to supply a worthy product of good quality to meet the increasing demand for such articles, a demand which, once an ample production is assured, may be enormously increased through a well-knit responsible organization such as here outlined as a series of

WORKSHOP AND EXHIBIT CENTERS established in various parts of the territory and integrated as a FEDERATION OF ALASKAN NATIVE ARTS.

This FEDERATION should be planned as a series of individual cooperatives, (directed during its formative period of 3 to 5 years, within which trial period limited title should be extended to each Center through the Native Alaskan Service) by a

CENTRAL ALASKAN MUSEUM in Juneau. In such a museum should be concentrated the direction of the workshop and exhibit centers.

It would add a much needed cultural importance and attraction (non-political) to the Capital. Natives and visitors should be able to realize and take part in Alaska's art background and traditions. When a museum is not a live and integral part of the life of a community, it might as well consider itself a mere storeroom. The Museum of Modern Art, for example, has achieved essential usefulness to the American Community.

The museum in Juneau would be indispensable as a guiding center for the development and constant improvement of living native arts which will eventually be of economic importance to Alaska, a credit and added interest to life in that territory.

The Central Alaskan Museum then, should be the seat of the Federation of Alaskan Native Crafts. It should contain all material available on arts native to Alaska, either acquired as part of its permanent collection or on loan. (The Rasmussen Collection, presently offered for sale, would form an indispensable nucleus). From this material, or on loan from other collections, either from the United States or abroad, traveling exhibits, small ones, should be formed and constantly circulated throughout the territory through the WORKSHOP AND EXHIBIT CENTERS.

Public cooperation for the establishment of this Central Museum will not be lacking. Contrary to previously formed impressions, this writer found, in his brief visit to Alaska, a very lively interest among individuals of various civic organizations toward such a build-up of Alaskan Art and Alaskan handcraft production. Teachers, members of Women's Clubs, Elks, Rotarians, Lions, newspaper editors, and members of Chambers of Commerce, as well as members of the Governmental Alaska Development Board, all showed a very real interest. Various of them were ready to suggest means for at least partially financing the development. It should be kept in mind that the Government has already a well-established bureau for the handling and marketing of native crafts.

One of the prime functions of the Central Alaskan Museum should be to publish and publicise all material of interest to or having to do with Alaskan Native Crafts.

Incidentally, the immediate printing of a non-technical but thoroughly illustrated series of catalogues in a uniform size would produce among the natives of Alaska a revivifying effect and a most fecund influence on and for their future production. These catalogue-like publications could be inexpensively bound and comprise, in a half dozen slender volumes, a small reference library on Alaskan Arts and Crafts. Subjects such as "20 Animals From Tlingit Carvings" - containing that many first rate full-page photographs, some in color (only details) from totemsñ or "20 Great Examples of Early Alaskan Indian and Eskimo Art", etc., etc. These little books should be put out from time to time under the imprint of the Central Alaskan Museum and not as Government pamphlets. They would not only fill a very real need of the Alaskan native for material from which to draw but would help him to see with his own eyes what has been done with his same material in the past.

They would most certainly meet with a ready market, not only with tourists, but in book markets, and form a dignified (and the first important) step in the process of culture pûblicity for Alaska in general.

The attention of thinking people should be directed to Alaska. A healthy interest in what is native to Alaska would be developed. And the younger and working elements among the Alaskan natives should be stimulated into production.

As the writer has noted the strong sympathy he found among the various civic organizations and other elements in Alaska toward any movement which would put the native crafts on a concrete footing, it should be made clear that at that time the plan herein contained had not been laid out.

Aside from elements mentioned, the writer firmly believes that the Central Museum and the Federation of Alaskan Native Art Centers herein outlined could be perfectly evolved under the fostering influence of the very strong organization already constituted as the Alaskan Native Service by the Department of the Interior. The Alaskan Native Service is at present rendering a complete social service to the native elements in Alaska in a most thorough-going manner (and with a minimum of personnel elements with which to work). Needless to say, the Alaskan Native Service is regarded by the vast majority of the natives there as a paternal, all powerful organization from which only good can be expected, because it represents for them a most constructive element. They have seen everything that it is doing in long range construction for a future state, including the building of future citizens.

Though the visit this writer made to Alaska was brief, he had an excellent opportunity to observe these things (from outside-in) throughout all south-east, south-central, and south-west and north-west Alaska. He talked with archaeologists, and with the chiefs and priests of the Islanders, with the Eskimos at Wales, and with George Ahgapuk at Shismaref, visited the tribal houses in Klukwan, Wrangell, and so on.

The Department of the Interior is strong with the native elements. In Brotherhoods and Sisterhoods of the Tlingkits, and Haidas, the Tsimshians, and the meeting houses, the Kazgas (or Kazins) on King Island, Little Diomede, and Nunivak are basic elements, the cooperation of which would help set up the units of the Workshop and Exhibit Centers.

The Function of the Government in this project would be merely that of architect for the structure and as a sponsor and balancing agent during a 3 or 5 year period of formation, providing the small financing necessary for inexpensive buildings and for the little machinery (buffers, sewing machines, etc.) necessary until the first, say three, Workshop and Exhibit Centers, were running autonomously.

Eventually, and probably within a period of three years, these first three centers should prove themselves in such manner as to warrant the extending of such a Federation to 12 or 15 other of the more or less isolated communities in Alaska.

The Function of the Workshop and Exhibit Center would be concentrated in two departments under one roof:

(a) an exhibit-salesroom, used for lectures and discussion groups, for the showing of illustrated material and rotating exhibits, instruction on methods, cine, for meetings, and as an attraction for the public and retail sales. In charge there should be a paid local secretary of the Federation who would also be in charge of the

(b) workshop, back of the exhibition (space or room), dedicated to the production of crafts which by tradition or because of materials native to the region would be worked there. Since none of the crafts concerned require other than the simplest machinery, five hundred to one thousand dollars should amply provide the equipment for one of these workshops.

Such a center established in such cities as Wrangell, Anchorage or Nome should become a warm and attractive focusing point, not only for the older workers, already specialists in their crafts, but for younger elements and apprentices who therein might find a life career.

At the same time it would solve the problem of winter occupation and a plan for workers who are at present engaged only in summer activities.

Well managed, these centers should form a compact, well-knit organization, a series of points at which specialized instruction might be imparted with a minimum of personnel. Periodically a mission of one or two specialists in carving, goldsmithing, sewing and so forth might visit and talk to them, and at the same time short talks and movies by writers or other distinguished local or visiting specialists would aid to broaden his sense of possibilities for the native and to shape individual development in right directions through constructive criticisms.

The strength of the organization of the Central Museum with its Federation of Alaskan Native Arts and its various Workshop and Exhibit Centers, would be multiple and cumulative, as in a chain of stores, or as with the various chapters of a Guild. The problem of seasonal activities is not peculiar to Alaska. The Swedes, in 1900, through its "Svensk Hemsloyd" solved their problem of "reconstituting winter employment" in a similar cooperative manner with results which have made that development world famous for its most excellent and valuable production.

The cooperative idea has already proven itself in Alaska as witness the community at Metlacatla, a community of some scarce 500 people. "The Apostle of Alaska", Father Duncan, though he died in 1918, founded a local organization so lively and so healthy that today, 28 years later, Metlacatla is probably the strongest community in Alaska, with a liquid reserve of over $500,000.00. (The manager's commission amounts to some $20,000.00 to $30,000.00 a year).

Under the absentee ownership condition, the greater part of the wealth produced in Alaska by the two major industries, fishing (one of the smaller cities mans 1800 boats) and mining, tends to leave the territory. Were mining and fishing removed, Alaska would become tomorrow a wasteland.

For every man who produces consumer goods in Alaska (aside from fishing and mining) there are probably twenty producing consumer goods for Alaska outside the territory. A great part of the wealth in Seattle alone has been formed by goods produced there for Alaskan consumption.

The fact that Alaskan ivory is more exquisitely and more cheaply carved in Seattle (as formerly in Japan) than in Alaska should be corrected without delay. This, and other tendencies, if not promptly counteracted, will result in another three years time in a senseless machine quantity production and cheapening of worthy and valuable native materials. They will be sold on the counters of chain drug stores. Their intrinsic possibilities will be vulgarized and lost to Alaska where they rightfully should be produced, by hand and by people whose heritage is the working of them.

Admittedly no art, (nor any business, for that matter) can stop still in one place without becoming stagnant. It must improve and fill new needs. There must be a constant effort to produce a finer article.

In line with this same thought and since it has been said that "the superior craftsman is the one who recognizes a superior tool when he sees one", the use of modern methods should not be withheld from the development of these small industries in Alaska. The technical knowledge of the worker should be reinforced and any menas of broadening the craftsman's sense of possibilities in the use of his material should be made available to him.

About the development of craftsmen. Although a group such as the King Islanders may be considered almost a guild, a center for craftsmanship where the craftsmen are already formed, it should be remembered that there are other parts of Alaska where such highly favorable conditions do not exist.

> In parts of southeastern Alaska there is an almost utter lack of younger elements learning to be craftsmen. This condition must be remedied and since in these parts today there are to be found only vestiges of former arts, the work of the Workshop and Exhibit Center must be intensified. The few that know how should be the ones to train large groups of apprentices, their knowledge should be utilized, and they should be paid as instructors. The future of the craftsmen of Alaska depends on the development of the young.
>
> There should be a constant flow of apprentices into these workshops, and a constant weeding out. Boys of 14 or even 12 years should be afforded the opportunity to acquire knowledge of a craft. Some will show an inherent aptitude for delicate carvings or for engraving or drawing, while others will develop a tendency or liking for the business of tanning skins or the making of toys.
>
> The boy who has worked every years for four years before he is 18 (on even half time) has actually acquired a birthright and an insurance against nonempdoyment. During that period of four years he will have naturally gravitated to the trade for which he has a bent. In rare cases he may show talents which warrant his continuing with a college education. Similarly, many will show themselves worthy of nothing better than loading bricks.
>
> A yearly interchange of skilled craftsmen between Alaska and continental United States, and, especially, Mexico, should be established immediately.

For this reason it should be made attractive for apprentices in large numbers to be placed in the Workshops. This system has, for hundreds of years, in Mexico and other countries, supplied the trades with craftsmen. In Alaska the six long months of winter should provide a perfect period of training.

Instead of an "Art Superintendent of Schools," the head of the Central Museum of Alaska should be named to direct the work of the workshop and Exhibit Centers, as "Design Director" or "Design Consultant." He should have under him a "Technical Consultant." Together they should be able to feed the Workshops with ideas, design criticism and correction, and with technical suggestions in such a manner that within a year's time the crafts in the villages where such centers have been established should feel a notable improvement in design and technical quality. In less than three years production should show a sizeable increase in volume and the Workshop Centers should be able to fill orders in quantities such as they never dreamed of previously, for markets which are always anxious for new and interesting native products.

The writer has seen a small town in Mexico where living a few years ago was on a hand-to-mouth basis and where Federal tax collections did not reach $50,000.00 pesos a year, and where, now, silversmiths, whose work formerly had scarce demand have seen their business bloom under the flow of orders from consumers' stores in the United States to a point where Federal tax collections last year reached more than $1,500,000.00 pesos. Where formerly the average craftsman was too poor to possess his own home, a goodly percentage of these same workers has now been able to acquire property and establish their family and become solid (tax-paying) members of the community.

In Alaska the writer found, among the eskimo and indian communities, that circumstances exist today very parallel to those that existed in Mexico ten years ago, the principal difference being merely that in Mexico, the indian population, contrary to the existing conditions in Alaska, is in the majority and that consequently in Mexico the Government has not been able to postpone its problem of social incorporation.

In Mexico, at least as far as the Government was concerned, discrimination between whites and native races has never existed. In Alaska the writer finds that even though a certain amount of discrimination admittedly exists in the streets of the Capital, even mention of such a thing diminishes in the smaller cities, and there were instances as in Wrangell, where the idea does not exist.

The logical conclusion is that, if the working eskimo and indian classes are to be absorbed as American citizens of equal potentialities, then the proposed Workshop and Exhibit Centers should seek the membership not only of the indians and eskimos, but of whites as well. (The whites or non-natives should not be discriminated against.) The eventual organization will be a stronger one and continue to grow.

It follows that the buildings for these Workshops and Exhibit Centers should be designed in such a way that they may be added to, (wood, the traditional building material, may now be fireproofed with a spray), and with the idea in mind of passing over to them a great deal of the "manual training" instruction which is as the present being imparted in various schools and which already overlaps to a degree. There seems to be no reason why school credit should not be given for training which will take place in the Workshop Center.

While the traditions and materials prevailing locally should more or less determine the type of work to be developed in each Workshop and Exhibit Center, it follows therefore that each Center should plan to become known and famous for only one or two types of product.

At the same time, it should be kept in mind that while certain design-elements and general design character in Alaska are to a degree interrelated, this fact contributes a sufficiently common interest as to bind these various Centers into a Federation. The fact that they will enjoy a common market, (certainly the export marketing which already is functioning through the wholesale department for native crafts of the Indian Affairs handles most efficiently the little material now produced) also serves to unify the Centers.

A tentative project for three Centers with which to commence the Federation might be laid out as follows (actual cities to be designated by Central Museum Board of Directors):

WRANGELL . . . . Wood
Lacquer

Furniture and cabinet-making. Rugged frontier type, not "Mission" but corresponding to that type, with hide seats, heavy plank tables, etc.

Toys. Without reproducing totems, the same spirit and elements of those carvings of animals, etc. (Perhaps one of Disney's men might collaborate the development). Alaskan toys should eventually enjoy a greater vogue than those formerly imported from Germany.

Home furnishings, such as lamps, kitchenware, bowls, trays, etc., articles which with the use of a finer lacquer than now used on the traditional Tlinguit pieces, could be executed in the same earthly colors and thus bring out a product completely Alaskan and of fresh interest.

ANCHORAGE . . . . Ceramics
Skins
Sewing

Anchorage is rapidly becoming an agricultural, shipping and fur center. Clay, for pottery and brick, exists there and a potential consumer's market.

NOME . . . . Ivory
Gold

The writer was strongly impressed by the ivory, of exeellent quality considering their limited technical means, which is worked in None during the four months of the summer by the King Islanders. These people work as a group and are entirely dedicated to their craft.

Gold, as a material for manufacture of fine articles, has never been developed in Alaska, though its combination with yellow ivory should form a very distinguished and valuable product, properly designed and executed. The connotation for gold with Alaska already exists and its combination with ivory should produce something distinguished and outstanding in Alaskan Arts and

Crafts. If two or three King Islanders, already skillful carvers, were sent as an interchange of students to Mexico, in six months they could start work in the Nome Workshop and Exhibit Center and with the apprentices they would train, in two years should be creating fine things, a product to add luster to the name of Alaska.

The above is merely a hint of the possibilities. Like Wrangell, Anchorage and Nome, there are certainly a score of cities or villages in Alaska, all more or less isolated, which, onee they became aware of what such centers were achieving for their communities, would take the initiative in establishing their own Centers within the Federation. (Anchorage was already requesting the repetition of a Crafts exhibit which had been organized by the Womens' Club at the time this writer was visiting Juneau.

NOTES:

(1) TRADITIONAL MATERIALS FOR INDUSTRIES PERTINENT AND NATIVE TO ALASKA.

Ivory carving - Bethel north to Barrow - ample supply.
Skin sewing (fur parkas have been produced in quantity during the war for armed forces.)
Basketry - (Fibres and whale-bone) Wales to Barrow and the Aleutians.
Wood carving - (Totem poles and ceremonial pieces). South-east. General.
Weaving - (Chilkat) Northern South-east material and weavers scarce.
Stone - (Argelite) carving. Material scarce, found only on Queen Charlotte Island.
Mocassin making, etc., etc.

(2) NEW INDUSTRIES ESSENTIAL (COMPLEMENTARY) TO ABOVE, AS YET PRACTICALLY NON-EXISTENT IN ALASKA.

Goldsmithing
Stone cutting (lapidaries)
Cabinet making (furniture)
Tanning
Pottery
Dressmaking

(3) BASIC MATERIALS PRESENT BUT ALMOST TOTALLY UNUTILIZED FOR

Wood pulp
Brick
Lime
Jade (Jade mountain above Kotzebue)
Marble (Tokeen)

Of these materials, groups I and II are important for the Workshop Centers and lend themselves to an immediate development.

Group III concerns material for less skilled manual labor,more properly within the sphere of small business and these materials are mentioned here merely to emphasize the grave lack of such basic material in Alaska. (Freight on a brick to Alaska is approximately twenty-five cents).

It will be noted by anyone who knows Alaska that this last group includes the industries which, though their production will be considered an essential and basic one in almost any community in the world, in Alaska they do not exist. (Brick, lime, etc.).

At the same time there are one or two crafts listed under "traditional industries" which, either for lack of material or for lack of people still versed in the manufacture, will probably be found undesirable to attempt to revive at the moment. However, this is merely a personal assumption. A person equipped with the proper enthusiasm and means (and personality) could perhaps manage to revive the weaving of Chilkat blankets, or the Chilkat type of weaving applied to other articles, which would in the long run justify his efforts.

The black stone, (argelite) which was formerly carved so beautifully by the Haida Indians, could be revived were the materials available. Perhaps the territorial government could arrange with Canada for the importation of some of this from Queen Charlotte Island, where it is principally found. In Hydaburg there are at least two excellent carvers of this stone, both Haida Indians, Sam Davis and John Walllace.

It might be wiser perhaps, under this plan, to shelve arts such as these which at the present moment exist as mere remnants, for a possible revival at a later date.

About Production of goods for tourist consumption: In the past few years, Mexicans, South Americans and others have had to learn that for the average visitor the necessity to acquire and take back native goods is an actual, lively urge to all travelers, almost without exception. The flow of tourists to Alaska has hardly begun. There is little conception there of the volume this trade will eventually produce. As a parallel development and along with this coming tourist trade, there will be buyers for the stores which will represent a more important and constant trade, i.e., the supplying of retail outlets in the United States and abroad.

It is the contention of the writer that articles which, due to form, material, or background, belong to the territory and which are normally produced there, are more certain of a long range market and are incidentally more attractive to the tourist than goods produced exclusively as "souvenirs" and in repetitious or consciously cheapened types.

In other words, since craft production in Alaska is practically beginning with a clean slate, the aim should be for primarily a normal trade in useful and fine objects, - not with the immediate intention of satisfying a transitory tourist demand for "gadgets". In the end the tourist with any criteria, one who distinguishes, will invariably find more satisfaction in acquiring a pair of authentic mocassins, well-made and for actual use, than a pair cheaply made, with white fluff around the top and beads which spell "Alaska" across the toe.

Also, the native will find a readier market for a series of fine articles in beaten gold mounted with yellow ivory or Alaskan jade in a limited quantity and without competition at a good price, than he will find for a hundred thousand place-cards at 25 cents made of the same ivory in an article unworthy of such fine material.

If it is generally agreed that the continental United States cannot ever return to those circumstances which once made handcrafts possible (and attractive) there, on the other hand Alaskan natives due precisely to their physical and geographical circumstances, just as in Norway, Sweden, or Mexico, do lend themselves to a production of articles made on an intimate (manual) scale in isolated communities or homes.

If, in spite of their poverty, their remoteness and lack of stimulating contacts and with only casual or accidental sales, the native people of Alaska have retained their ability to produce in craft-form things which are still their own, there is no doubt that as distances are reduced by air traffic, and now that the benefits of medical service, good government and civic co-operation have reached them, that with intelligent planning these same crafts can become strong and productive economically for Alaska. All the elements are there. Only a planned structure is lacking.

WILLIAM SPRATLING.

October 1, 1945.
Taxco el Viejo, Gro.,
Mexico.

BIBLIOGRAPHY

Davis, Mary L. and Greta Pack. *Mexican Jewelry*. Austin: University of Texas Press, 1963.

De Crellana, Margarita. *Crafts of Mexico*. Washington DC: Smithsonian, 2004.

El Arte Popular de Mexico. Mexico D.F.: Artes de Mexico, 1970-71.

Figueroa, Leslie Cortes de. *Taxco, The Enchanted Hill Town*. Mexico, D.F.: 1960.

Flandrau, Charles Macomb. *Viva Mexico*. New York, N.Y.: D. Appleton and Company, 1910.

Grande Maestros of Arte Popular Mexicano, Mexico D. F.: Banamex, 1996.

Harvey, Marion and Ken Harvey. *Crafts of Mexico*. Mexico D. F.: G V Entores, 1997.

McMenamin, Donna. *Popular Arts of Mexico*. Atglen, Pennsylvania: Schiffer Publishing, 1996.

Mexico hecho a mano-centro. Mexico D. F.: AM EDITORES S.A. DE C.V., 2007.

Mexico hecho a mano-sur. Mexico D. F.: AM EDITORES S.A. DE C.V., 2008.

Mexico hecho a mano-norte. Mexico D. F.: AM EDITORES S.A. DE C.V., 2009.

Morrill, Penny Chittim. *William Spratling and the Mexican Silver Renaissance*. New York, N.Y.: Harry C. Abrams, 2002

———. *Silver Masters of Mexico*. Atglen, Pennsylvania: Schiffer Publishing, 1996.

———. and Carol A. Berk. *Mexican Silver: Modern Hand-wrought Jewelry and Metalwork*. Atglen, Pennsylvania: Schiffer Publishing, 4th Edition, 2007.

Rothstein, Arden and Anya Rothstein. *Mexican Folk Art*. Atglen, Pennsylvania: Schiffer Publishing, 2007.

Sayer, Chloe. *Crafts of Mexico*. Garden City, New Jersey: Double Day & Co., Inc., 1977.

———. *Arts & Crafts of Mexico*. San Francisco, California: Chronicle Books, 1990.

Spratling, William. *File on Spratling, An Autobiography*. Boston: Little, Brown & Company, 1967.

———. *More Human than Devine*. Mexico D. F.: Universidad Nacional Autonoma de Mexico, 1960.

———. and William Faulkner. *Sherwood Anderson and Other Famous Creoles*. Austin, Texas: University of Texas, 1966.

———. *The Popular Art of Mexico*. 4th Edition, Mexico D. F.: Arte de Mexico, 1979.

INDEX

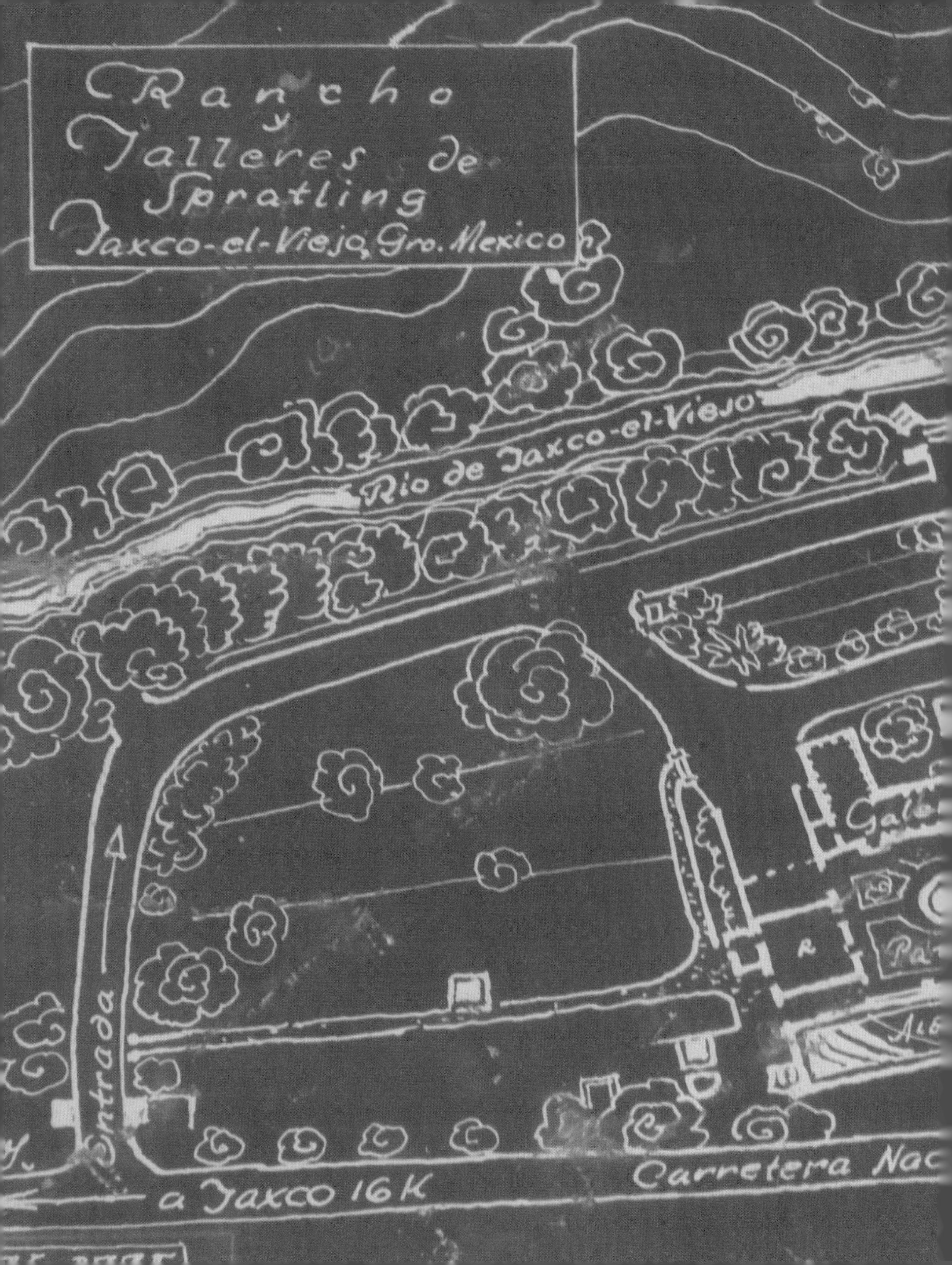
Rancho
y
Talleres de
Spratling
Taxco-el-Viejo, Gro. Mexico
Rio de Taxco-el-Viejo
Entrada
a Taxco 16 K
Carretera Nac